More Praise for
What They Didn't Expect When They Were Expecting
. . . And How They Became Better Parents

"Somewhere between 'I do' and 'We're gonna have a baby!' and certainly long before the first 'No!' is shouted in defiance, couples need to establish happy, healthy working relationships. This book clearly outlines just how that can be done. It also explains how your kids affect your marriage and how your marriage affects your kids. I really do wish I'd had a copy of this given to me as a wedding gift!"
—**GWEN EATON MCCONNELL, R.N.**
Obstetric nurse

"What They Didn't Expect When They Were Expecting helped me to reevaluate my role(s) within my marriage, increase communication, abandon previous misconceptions and create what I've found to be a much more supportive and healthy family environment for my wife, children, and myself."
—**JOSHUA HART**
Manager at Lowe's

"Dr. Leslie's book reminds new parents about how important it is to reflect not just upon their role of mother or father but also upon their roles as partners and individuals. For the exhausted new parent, such advice is crucial to helping promote balance in a life that can feel suddenly and overwhelmingly focused on children."
—**JASON LATOUCHE, PH.D.,**
Assistant Professor of Sociology
Tarleton State University

Praise for Dr. Leslie's seminars

Book Dr. Leslie for your church or civic group:

Dr.Leslie@hotmail.com

What They Didn't Expect When They Were Expecting

. . . AND HOW THEY BECAME BETTER PARENTS

By

DR. LESLIE STANLEY-STEVENS

For Christopher

CONTENTS

Part I: Great Expectations

Part II: Paradise Lost

Part III: No Man or Woman Is an Island

Part IV: The Sun Also Rises

Great Expectations

Introduction

Kid Pro Quo

Have you ever gone on a trip and upon arrival said, "This isn't what I thought it would look like"? And when asked what you expected, you reply, "I don't know." It's a common experience. We have an idea in our mind's eye but when we see reality, the imaginary loses focus. I find this phenomenon so fascinating that I like to ask my family what they are expecting before we arrive, while we can still describe what we're imagining. A bonus to this game with young children is they are just not as bound to reality as we are, so the beaches have dragons and the mountains are rainbow-colored. My kids are now teenagers who have more realistic expectations of our travel venues. But our recent trip to the Grand Canyon revealed how being "realistic" doesn't always make our expectations accurate. The pictures we saw before we went didn't capture the magnitude of that landscape and words were no match for our footsteps into its vast grandeur. Over the years, we've found our real vacation destination is sometimes better, sometimes worse, sometimes just as good—but always different (and, so far, no dragons).

What is true about vacation expectations is true about our families as well. We learn about our expectations by bringing them to the forefront of our minds, often by discussing them with others. This book is for people—women and men—who want to have a child and have the good sense to give it some thought before the child is born. Having children is such a blessing but it also can be very hard. Many of the difficulties that result from the birth or adoption of a child can be reduced through thinking and planning. In addition, this book will help people in the throes of raising young children and trying to balance paid work, childcare and housework. Even if one parent doesn't work for pay, a balance between the parents is still necessary.

The name of this introduction is *Kid Pro Quo*, playing on the Latin *quid pro quo*, (literally "something for something") suggesting trade-offs—I scratch your back, you scratch mine. There are many trade-offs with work and family. Not only do parents need to trade off between the two of them as they try, as a unit, to provide financially, emotionally, and physically for themselves and their children, but there's a trade-off between work and family as well. People need work to provide financially for themselves and their families and also to meet some deep-seated personal needs for identity and feelings of contribution to the greater society.[1] However, work can also be a royal pain in the neck. One reason is we tend to do too much of it. Another is it usually requires time away from our families—sometimes running directly against our family's needs. For instance, we may have to forego school programs because of our jobs. Other times, we have to uproot and move our families in order to work.

The trade-off between work and family means that work needs family too. The workplace depends on families to provide good employees. First, employers expect that their workers have values that make them honest, productive and "play well with others"—people learn good values in the family more than anywhere else. Also, the workplace depends on families to meet the physical needs of their employees such as with meals, laundry, and rest. Lastly, the workplace expects families to be a source of emotional support. Families help their members deal with personal issues, and sometimes they even provide support for conflicts people have at work.

While, ideally, families provide nurture and stability, sometimes they require work sacrifices. For instance, a child is born and the worker needs to take time off to bond with him or her, or that child is sick and the worker has to take a sick day. Sometimes workers change jobs entirely, in order to be more present to their families. Unfortunately, the time when our work requires the most of us (early in our careers) is also the time our families require the most (when our children are young). This book addresses the complexities of successfully navigating our needs through this difficult period.

What We Need

There's a bumper sticker that says, "If Momma Ain't Happy, Ain't Nobody Happy." Ain't it the truth! And it's true for Papa too! The well-being of one family member affects all the rest. Happiness is contagious—and by happy, I mean that general feeling of contentedness with life. Happy people tend to establish good relationships with their families. Momma and Papa are more likely to be happy if they have worked out a good relationship between the two of them before the first child comes along—which is one of the most unsettling of life events. Becoming happy parents requires that we address our own needs and wants from the start to ensure that we have a happy family both now and in the future. One of the ways we can ease the transition to parenthood is to pay attention to the expectations we have. Premarital counseling helps with this process.

Good premarital counseling requires the prospective spouses to describe their anticipated roles of husband and wife, for themselves and their spouse. This same couple will need to reconsider these roles as they consider parenthood. They need to discuss details such as

- **Who will be responsible for getting up during the night? Will we share that role?**
- **Will someone stay at home? If so, how will we decide who stays at home?**
- **Will our jobs be equally important?**
- **Who will take off work when the baby is sick?**
- **Will we both take maternity/paternity leave? For how long?**
- **Do we both have equal "say-so" in how these decisions are being made?[2]**

Having our relationship with our spouse well established before that first child comes along frees the parents to focus on the child's needs and to enjoy them more.[3] It's no surprise that children are better adjusted when their parents are getting their own needs met and are in a loving, committed relationship with one another. When the parents function as a team, they gain support from each other both during the good times and during the trials of raising children.

This book uses Bowen's Family Systems Theory to provide a helpful framework to use in making strong love relationships. Family Systems Theory is easy to learn and it is flexible enough to work with wide differences in our personal experiences. No wonder it's a popular theory for counselors working with families and with sociologists who are studying them. To begin, every person has needs for closeness (WE) and the need for space or independence (ME). Considering married couples, we have two sets of these needs going on and these needs should be kept in balance. I am going to refer to this concept as ME-WE-ME.[4]

Additionally, each of us has our own sets of hopes, needs, and aspirations. These stay important even when we are in close relationships with others. Central to our well-being is the question, "Can I still be me while being close to you?" In a good marriage, each person is aware of his/her own hopes, needs, and aspirations as well as her/his spouse's hopes, needs, and aspirations.

There are several common ways that ME-WE-ME can get out of balance. First, sometimes there can be too much ME in the relationship. Each person is so involved in his/her own hopes needs, and aspirations that there is not enough emphasis on togetherness. The couple isn't putting their time into the relationship. We can refer to these relationships as centrifugal because all of the energy is spinning outside of the relationship— much like what happens to children as the centrifugal force pulls them away from the center of a merry-go-round. Sometimes these marriages end up in divorce. Other times, the people stay married but are somewhat alienated from each other, getting their needs met in other ways, for instance through work or through affairs. It would be imprudent to actually speculate about individual couples but, as an example, the information the media provide about high-profile movie stars' love lives and how seldom they seem to stay together suggests these centrifugal approaches. Too involved with their work and with themselves, these people don't provide the kind of nurturance a good relationship requires.

A second way ME-WE-ME can be out of balance is with too much WE. Directing all of their energies inward, these relationships can be referred to as "centripetal." Centripetal relationships neglect relationships outside of the marital bond. Consequently, the individuals often lose the perspective provided by distance from their mate and the insights other relationships offer. The individuals in centripetal relationships lean so heavily on one another that they can't stand on their own very well, which is why such couples are often described as "codependent." Ironically, codependent couples often think of their closeness as a strength in their relationship.

One problem that sometimes happens in relationships with too much WE is that the WE actually looks like one of the people's ME. In other words, the two have become one, and the one is not a blend of the two of them. Let me give you an illustration. In the movie *The Accidental Tourist*, Macon Leary comes home to hear his wife, Sarah, tell him she wants a divorce. She says, "I'm becoming a Leary."

Macon scoffs and says, "There are worse things than that."

Sarah responds, "Not for me." You see, Leary is his birth name, not hers. It's fine for him to be a Leary because it is his ME. But what Sarah is communicating throughout their conversation is that she has quit having her own responses to situations and is only seeing the world through his eyes. She's lost her sense of self and she needs to get it back. He doesn't see the problem because he hasn't lost his sense of self.

Yet a third way ME-WE-ME can get out of kilter is with a distancer-pursuer dance. These couples have one person who needs more closeness (WE) than the other person desires. The pursuer keeps trying to get closer and the distancer keeps moving away, assuring that about the same amount of distance is kept in the relationship. This is a tiresome way to live. It's frustrating, perhaps for both parties but, especially for the pursuer who might finally get fed up and stop. At this point, the distancer might be glad and keep going or she/he might say, "Hey, wait a minute," and turn around and start pursuing. The former pursuer may be glad and they finally work things out or she/he may say, "Too little, too late, bucko."

Lastly, power imbalances can inhibit family functioning. When one person has more power in the relationship than the other, that person's ME is taking precedence over the other's. Imbalances in power reduce the intimacy (emotional closeness) in the relationship. In such situations, persons without as much power tend to withhold information for fear of getting hurt. Once children come along, they tend to feel closer to the parent with lesser power, disclosing information to this parent with pleas such as, "Don't tell Dad."[5] Equally shared power provides the greatest intimacy with partners, where both persons are equally available to the other, encouraging and supporting their spouse's hopes, needs, and aspirations.[6]

Both people in the couple need to have a life of their own before they can appropriately merge into a successful WE. Ideally the couple will have worked out a good balance of ME-WE-ME by the time the first child comes along because that will be a new ME to add to the family WE.

How the Book Is Set Up

This book reports on real people—women and men—who were expecting their first child. I surveyed and interviewed almost 100 first-time, expectant mothers and fathers to learn about what they expected of their work and family experiences. Some of these individuals were planning their families in great detail, while others were surprised by the pregnancies. Some had specific career goals, while others planned to stay at home with their children. I interviewed many of these parents again when their oldest children were about five years old. While their expectations and desires varied, they all found their expectations differed from reality. On the pages that follow, I describe the common experiences of expectant parents and the realities that result. I also describe how individuals and couples work through their needs for togetherness (WE) and their needs for space (ME).

The first part of the book describes what these young couples think parenting will be like and how they plan to divide paid work, housework and childcare (see Part I "Great Expectations," Chapters 1 and 2). It also describes some of the factors—such as family background—influencing their ideals about how they want things to be. Part II, playfully titled "Paradise Lost," includes Chapters 3, 4 and 5 in which these same mothers and fathers describe life now that their oldest children are four or five years old. Chapter 3 reveals "What They Didn't Expect When They Were Expecting." Interestingly, having children threatens the balance of

ME and WE. One or both parents can start investing too much in work, for instance. These imbalances are discussed in Chapter 4—"Rebalancing the ME-WE-ME"—and in Part IV, "The Sun Also Rises." Chapter 5—"Winning Teams: What Makes the Most Successful Families"—describes the common characteristics of the families that were balancing work and family the most successfully.

In Part III of the book, "No Man or Woman Is an Island," I address how the culture around us influences our decisions and values. Chapter 6 focuses on work and the American work culture, including its toll on families. Work is an essential element in our lives. Not only do we "gotta eat," but work (at its best) also provides feelings of accomplishment and fulfillment. This chapter also addresses the effective use of paid childcare. "Seeing is Believing" (Chapter 7) explores messages in movies and television, focusing on how they shape and reflect our culture's values, which affect our own choices.

The last section of the book, "The Sun Also Rises," describes practical solutions for the dilemmas of American working families, whether one parent or both are in the workforce. Chapter 8—"Every Home Is a Home School"—discusses the impact of our decisions regarding work and family on our children. I also present common "problem scenarios" and workable solutions as we move toward our goal of meeting the needs of each person in our families. Consequently, this chapter includes a section on discipline. Chapter 9 provides practical tips for expectant and new parents, while Chapter 10 provides the actual survey and interview questions used in this study so that readers can answer them too, and compare their answers to those in the book.

My experience as a wife, mother and university professor of sociology sparked my interest in the topics in this book. Throughout my career, I have focused my attention on the American family and I share much that I have learned in the pages that follow. In addition to reporting on the parents I surveyed and interviewed, I also share information my students have found helpful in their own lives as they ponder the challenges of their families in this modern age. Throughout the book I use my research in the area of how work affects families as well as the experience which seventeen years of teaching my favorite course, "Sociology of the Family," provides.

Chapter 1

21ˢᵗ Century Fathers

The Legacy of Ward Cleaver, Tim Taylor, and Cliff Huxtable

With his panda eyes, Greg looks tired. I'm glad he could find time for this interview. As a hospital lab technician, Greg expects to continue working ten-hour shifts, four days a week, after their baby is born and may start working more. His wife, Gretchen, a nutritionist, is going to stay home full time. Greg reveals these details methodically, reflecting his personality and the approach he and Gretchen have taken to planning their family.

Greg was one of twenty-five first-time expectant fathers I studied regarding their expectations about fatherhood and balancing work and family[7] (see Table 3 in Chapter 10). It only makes sense that the addition of a child to the WE of a marriage requires some adjustment to a man's sense of ME. As these men anticipated their new roles of fathers, their roles as workers and husbands figured prominently. Most of these men worked between forty and fifty hours a week and planned to work slightly more once their children were born. They didn't expect that their families would cause any negative effects on their careers.

Greg and Gretchen waited until both were out of college and had established their young careers before buying a house and trying to have a baby. Now they are conscientiously cutting down on their expenses so that they can live on one salary when the baby comes. Choosing to have Gretchen stay at home with the child reflects some of the more traditional values both fathers and mothers expressed during the interviews. But Greg and Gretchen are unique in that they have put so much forethought, planning, and action into supporting these values.

Slightly more than half of the men in my study worked for companies which had some sort of "family-friendly" policies such as paternity leave and flextime. However, only 23 percent of the fathers with these options planned to take advantage of them. For example, the men were not planning to take advantage of family (or paternity) leave after the birth of their child even when such leave was available. Rather, they planned to take an average of 7.6 *vacation* days because that's what their coworkers do.[8] Even when the companies offer paternity leave, if most men are not taking it, others are reluctant to do so for fear of looking like they're not committed to their jobs. One has to wonder just how "family-friendly" the policies really are if employees are unwilling to use them!

By only taking a few days off after their babies are born and increasing their work hours, most men communicated the importance of breadwinning in their perception of what it meant to be a good father. But the men gave less traditional opinions when asked how they felt about mothers working. Most thought that having a mother who worked had either a positive effect or no effect on the child's well being, social development, and cognitive development (see Table 4 in Chapter 10). These views aren't surprising since about half of the men had mothers who worked when they were young and had seen for themselves that it didn't have detrimental effects, not to mention they recognized the benefits of her income. Even some of the men whose mothers did not work when they were young saw the benefits of working mothers and had wives who planned to work once their children were born.

The fourteen men I talked to in-depth tended to resemble one of three fathers they had watched on TV while they were growing up: *Leave It to Beaver's* Ward Cleaver (reflecting traditional values), *Home Improvement's* Tim the Tool Man Taylor (combining traditional values with a new emphasis on involvement with the children), and *The Cosby Show's* Cliff Huxtable (equally sharing work and family responsibilities with their wives). Half of the interviewees resembled Ward Cleaver, five were like Tim the Tool Man, and two were like Cliff Huxtable.

Ward Cleaver: The Traditional Man

When asked "what does fatherhood mean to you," men who emphasized the breadwinner role as their highest priority were categorized as traditional. Like TV's Ward Cleaver, these men invest a bulk of their time into their jobs or careers and leave most of the domestic work to their wives. Typically, they planned to take zero to three days off when their child is born and then expected to increase their weekly work hours after that.

Like Ward, the traditional men performed only a minimum amount of domestic work, such as yard and automotive work, while assuming a helper capacity with regard to housework and child rearing.

How these men were raised hugely affected their plans for their new families. They all came from traditional families, with their fathers being the primary breadwinners and most of their mothers staying home until the interviewees were at least school age. Despite their desire to follow in their father's footsteps, only two of these Ward Cleavers had wives who would be staying home full time. So, ironically, for most of these Wards, their wife is not June Cleaver since she has added the traditional male breadwinner role to her plate. Even so, the Ward Cleavers didn't intend to return the favor by doing more of the traditionally female domestic roles like washing those plates.

THE WARD CLEAVER TYPES

- ♦ **7 have traditional gender role expectations for themselves**
- ♦ **7 came from traditional household structures**
- ♦ **4 say housework and childcare should be shared equally when both spouses work fulltime**
- ♦ **0 currently share housework equally with their wives who were working fulltime**
- ♦ **2 have wives who will stay home once the baby is born**

Another funny thing about the Ward Cleaver types is that, even though four of the seven believed childcare and domestic duties should be shared equally when both parents work fulltime, they didn't actually share housework equally even before the baby arrived. They also expressed what appeared to be lip-service regarding plans for the future. Consider Henry, a nineteen-year-old manual worker whose wife volunteered him for this study. Both of them were interviewed at their upstairs apartment where they had moved just a few months earlier.

Interviewer: *How do you and your wife share housework?*
Henry: *She does a lot of it. I realize I should do more, but, I guess . . . I don't.*
Interviewer: *Will that change after the baby is born?*
Henry: *(Pause) I'm going to try and do a lot more.*

Some such as Peter, a twenty-seven-year-old construction worker, divide chores along traditionally gendered lines. Typical "manly" jobs like repairs and yard work aren't tasks you do daily, while cooking, cleaning, and childcare are never ending. Such a split makes more sense if the man is the sole breadwinner and the woman's "job" is the housework and childcare. However, keeping that split when the wife is in the workforce truly exemplifies the notion of, "A man will work from to sun to sun but a woman's work is never done." Since they are the ones who are twice as likely to be pulling that vacuum out of the closet, working moms routinely get less sleep and less leisure time than their husbands.

Peter: *Usually I get everything outside and she gets every-thing inside, pretty much. But we help each other out. We're good about that. I help with dishes and stuff . . . odds and ends, whatever.*
Interviewer: *How do you feel about that?*
Peter: *It doesn't bother me at all. I enjoy doing stuff like that, I guess.*
Interviewer: *Will that change after the baby's born?*
Peter: *No I wouldn't think so . . . No, I wouldn't think so.*

Peter, whose wife teaches third grade, appears to think he's doing his fair share. Others who also claimed to share equally seemed to be taking a back seat because they couldn't name specifics. "It's pretty much 50-50. I think it's a great compromise," says Zack as he smoothes out his sandy hair. When I asked him to list his responsibilities, he added, "Mainly I take out the trash and clean up around the garage and outside and mow the yard and stuff like that." He doesn't expect that to change once the baby is born, which may suggest that he doesn't know how much work that baby is going to create!

Zack and the other traditional males' emphasis on breadwinning causes them to think in terms of working more for pay, not working more around the house in order to adjust to the presence of a new little family member. So, when asked if they would stay home if it were financially feasible, it caught these guys off guard. Many needed prompting on the question because they had never considered staying at home with their children while their wives worked. (Tim asked, "You mean, like, if I win the lottery?") They saw their pay as essential to their family's survival, but traditionalists said that they would work even if they could afford not to. Some of the men responded to the question about their staying home by saying they would like for *their wives* to stay home, reflecting how they could not consider such an option for themselves. "If I could afford not to work . . . I don't know. I probably couldn't do it," said Tim, who works full time while completing his college degree. "I would not feel that would be an appropriate thing for me to do. Well, the male stereotype, you know." Similarly, Zack felt that if he didn't work he would be "totally lost." These men keenly identify with the breadwinner role and rely on their careers for a large part of their personal fulfillment.   However, the other half of the men I interviewed were breaking out of this narrowly defined ideal of how to be a father.

Tim "The Tool Man" Taylor: Combining Breadwinning and Nurturing Roles

Like Tim the Tool Man from television's *Home Improvement,* men practicing the combination role add more of an emphasis on family involvement to their traditional values. The Tim Taylors prioritized their work over the work of their spouses and identified themselves primarily as breadwinners.[9] But these combination fathers contribute more than the Ward Cleavers to household labor and recognize that they need to do even more once the baby is born. Still, they don't come close to doing as much as their wives. Combination fathers also put more emphasis on family interaction, including childcare, and shared decision-making with their spouses. Therefore, Greg (described at the beginning of this chapter) is classified as combination because he already does half of the housework and because of his expectation to do more than half of the childcare on his three days off per week—"to give her a break" –even though he will be the sole breadwinner.

These men's own fathers' influences were extremely important in how they defined the role of fatherhood, either by providing a negative example or, as was the majority, providing a positive role model. Norm illustrates this point:

> *I learned from my father that he always valued time with us. Whenever he was not working, whenever he could get*

*away, he would . . . I knew that we were special. So, I think
seeing that, it's just automatic for me to want to do the same.*

Even though they thought highly of their fathers, the
Tim Taylors wanted to spend more time with their families than their own fathers had. For instance, Norm,
like Greg, planned for his wife to stay at home, yet he
appreciated the difficulties of taking care of children
full time and described how he would take over and give
his wife breaks on his days off. These attitudes reflect
a positive approach to helping their wives nurture their
ME—their hopes, needs and aspirations.

All of the Tim Taylors also reported that it is both the
mother's and the father's role to prioritize family over
career or work, but they varied on how important their
work was to them. When asked how he would feel about
staying home full time if he could afford it, Norm, a biologist at a commercial laboratory, said that if he didn't
work, he could be "totally consumed with my family" and
would not miss work. However, Roger, a manager of a
large retail store, felt that he would enjoy spending time
at home, but that eventually he would not have enough
to do: "I enjoy the accomplishment of work."

Cliff Huxtable: The Equal Sharers

The most interesting and dynamic of the father
interviews came from the excited men who illustrate
equally shared roles with their wives. Like Cliff and
Claire Huxtable of *The Cosby Show,* these couples made
decisions together. The Cliff Huxtables did not prioritize their work over their spouse's and spent as much
time with their hands in dirty dishwater as their wives.
Unlike the other fathers, they provided details for how

they would care for their infants, discussing such issues as diapers and car seats.

Coming from families with negative male role models, both of the Cliff Huxtables (Sid and Ike) had working mothers, and fathers who were not involved in their home lives or extracurricular activities. Determined to provide a good male role model, these men planned to be actively involved in their children's care. Both were also evangelical Christians. Past studies have reported that evangelical Christians were more likely to be traditionalists, leaning on the patriarchy of the Bible to support their position. [10] But Sid and Ike used their interpretations of the Bible to support more of a "servanthood" relationship to their families, causing them to want to be more involved in the relational aspects of family life. Their responses were visceral—I could see in their eyes and movements how close to their hearts paternal involvement was. Practically bouncing on his chair, Ike expressed it thusly:

> *In that my father chose to leave, I think they (his father's and his views of childcare) differ greatly. It's not about my life, it's about that child's life. I mean that child didn't choose to come into this world. That's my responsibility and it's about laying down my will so I can serve that kid, . . . that child, . . . my baby.*

Clearly, Ike is seeking to follow the example of Christ who said, "There is no greater love than to lay down one's life for one's friends" (John 15:13 NLT).

Of all the interviewees, only Sid and Ike said they wished their fathers had spent more time with them growing up. Now they plan to be the kind of fathers they wish they had had. "My father was a police officer too, and he worked basically the shift that I'm working," Sid explains. "He wasn't there a lot of times. If one of us could stay home, that'd be awesome. I mean, hey, I'd do it." Continuing with specifics about his desires he adds, "I don't know if she'd want me to tell you or not but my wife doesn't have a very strong stomach. So I told her, I plan on changing all the diapers."

In addition, both Sid and Ike voiced commitment to assisting their spouses in furthering their careers. That commitment was reflected in the ways they described sharing decision-making and by truly splitting domestic duties, giving their spouses more time to devote to work. Anticipating the added responsibilities of childcare, Ike and his wife, Isabel, worked out a plan where Ike will continue to work nights and take care of the baby during the day, and Isabel will attend classes during the day and take care of the baby at night. Indeed, the Cliff Huxtables most clearly articulated plans that would allow balance of the ME-WE-ME throughout the transition to parenthood.

Childcare

Three-quarters of the twenty-five survey respondents felt that childcare responsibilities should be shared equally when both parents work full time, and seventy-six percent also felt that housework should be shared equally. A majority of the interviewees expected to do more domestic work once the baby is born. However, most of their responses fell into the "helper" category in that they will rely on their spouses to direct what duties to perform. "I'm willing to do as much as she asks me," Norm says earnestly, leaning forward on the couch.

All of the traditionalists fell into the "helper" category. Being a helper, of course, requires that someone else is actually in charge. The term "helper" is very appropriate with respect to this role as every Ward Cleaver used the terms "help her" or "help out" with respect to domestic duties and childcare issues. This division of labor makes the most sense for the two Ward Cleavers whose wives will be at home full time, but those whose wives work full time may find that they need to be more involved in order to avoid having their wives be too overloaded.

The combination and egalitarian fathers already share domestic duties much more than the traditionalists, and they expect to pick up even more responsibility after the baby's birth. To summarize, although most of the to-be dads expect to have to do more domestic chores, they will simply be continuing their existing domestic duty arrangements: The egalitarian arrangements will continue to be egalitarian in nature, and the traditional arrangements will continue to be traditional.

Interestingly, of the fourteen interviewees, only three expressed their plans to interact with their children while the children were infants. Half did not address interacting with their children at all—even when asked how their lives would be different once their child is born. Most described the time off when their child is born as time to address the spouse's needs, again in a "helper" capacity, rather than as a time to get to know their babies. "Maybe a couple of days," says Zack. "I thought that maybe it would be helpful to my spouse and everything to take a few days off." Sharing Zack's perspective, Tim offers, "When the baby's first born, I'll probably take two to three days. She'll be off work, so I felt that it's probably best to help her get her, a full day's sleep probably—yeah, recuperating."

Only Ike and Sid talked about bonding with the child. Sid explains:

> *Because, you know, I want to be there for the birth and all that. I felt it (taking two weeks off) was needed time, like it's just as important for me to bond with the child as it is for my wife. There's already a special bond, right?-- that they're having right now. Actually, I feel it's make-up time for me. I mean she's nine months with the bonding. I feel when I'm starting I have nine months to make up. I know two weeks is not enough, but it's what I can afford to do right now.*

Others talked about sharing time with their children by involving the child in their own hobbies or in attending their children's school and extra-curricular functions. Two of the Ward Cleavers provide examples:

Interviewer: *How do you think your life will be different once your child is born?*

Vance: *There'll be, probably, less free time.*

Interviewer: *What about your hobbies and sports?*

Vance: *There'll still be time for that—I hunt and fish, my main hobbies, so I plan on teaching the kid how to hunt and fish.*

Jerry: *I love to fish and I could fish every weekend if I wanted to, but with a child, I know there's gonna come a time when you gotta go to track meets, you gotta go to basketball games, whatever, volleyball. And that'll change an aspect. I'll just focus more on her life and . . . still make her a good fisherman, one way or the other.*

It is fun to hear these guys describe how they will get their kids involved in their favorite activities. On top of that, it's exciting to hear how they plan to be involved with their girls as well as their boys. Obviously these men are considering how they will keep a sense of themselves (their ME) while incorporating a child into their lives. However, since these activities are well past the time of infancy and toddlerhood, it seems that many of the participants have not considered the time of infancy as a critical time for father-child interaction. In fact, they may not see themselves as instrumental in the development of their children during this time. Or, at least, these men haven't identified themselves fully as fathers yet, not visualizing life with a baby, except in terms of financial responsibility. Further, it appears that although parental roles are changing, these men still perceive the mother as most important during the time of infancy.

What We Can Learn From Expectant Fathers

Like the expectant mothers, the expectant fathers consider their own upbringing when imagining their new families. They desire to repeat the good and change the bad. Some men wanted to be like their fathers, thinking of their dads as good fathers even when most of what they had to say about them was that they worked a lot. Others didn't plan to work less than their dads but expected to do more with their children. This was often expressed by saying they would help their wives rather than through direct involvement or bonding with the child. The two fathers who came from divorced parents strongly wanted to be different from their fathers, saying they wanted to be there for their children and provide stability.

The men's strong affinity for their breadwinning roles when describing what it means to be a father might cause them to feel separated from their families: What makes them feel most like a good father is what they are doing away from their family. Ironically, many fathers stated that they want to be involved, good fathers, yet they were not planning to reduce paid work hours or take more than a few days off from work with the birth, even when the mothers work too. Some plan to increase paid work hours. Therefore, these men's notions of fathering do not appear to be associated with actual time with the child, especially the baby. Even when the children become older, the men talked about their involvement in terms of activities like fishing and going to games more than actual child care.

Additionally men's focusing on the breadwinning role may put unrealistic pressure on them since the U.S. economy often requires two earners for a family to be in the middle class. If a man measures himself against those who out earn him, he could continually feel like he needs to work more. It could also give him license to selfishly pursue his career (his ME) at the expense of his family (WE), and particularly at his wife's expense—she would be forced to shoulder more of the family responsibilities because someone has to take up the slack.

In all cases, these expectant fathers were affected profoundly by their reactions to their own upbringing. The following chapter describes the mothers' expectations.

QUESTION TO ASK YOURSELF AND DISCUSS

What kind of husband will you/your husband be? Ward? Tim? Cliff?

Chapter 2

All Mothers Work

How Expectant Mothers Decide About Paid Work

Diane shifts in the chair as if she's trying to move out from under the increasing weight eight months of pregnancy has produced. Anxiously looking forward to the birth of her child, she's always wanted to be a mother and she's thought through her decisions about work quite thoroughly. I first met Diane almost a decade ago when I began a study of 63 married women who were pregnant with their first babies. Like all the mothers I interviewed, she earnestly desired to be a good mother. Generally, I wanted to learn about their expectations of motherhood. I was particularly interested in finding out what these women were planning regarding whether they were going to work full-time for pay, work part-time for pay or stay at home once their babies were born. Additionally, I wanted to hear their thoughts on how they planned to share childcare and housework with their husbands. Lastly, I wanted to know what influenced their decision-making. For instance, how did their upbringing affect their viewpoints?   How much did family, friends, and spouses affect their positions? [11]

Throughout this chapter, I will discuss these expectant mothers' varying approaches regarding the sharing of paid work, housework, and childcare with their spouses.   These are crucial areas where new couples must balance their ME-WE-ME. First, let's look at what most strongly influenced women's decisions regarding work and family.

What Influences Women's Decisions?

When I first interviewed Diane, she was working at her dream job. Right out of high school, she set her sights on interior design. After she completed an internship, she had enjoyed building her client base over the last six years. Despite the love she had for her job and the tremendous effort she'd put into it, Diane now planned to quit in order to be a stay-at-home mom. But most of the other women chose to continue working when they enjoyed their jobs. Whether the women chose to work for pay or stay at home full time was based on many aspects of their own backgrounds and how they felt about their present situations. To investigate how the decisions were made, I, along with my research team,[12] asked our expectant mothers whether their own mothers worked or not, and how they felt about it. Additionally, we asked about what effects they thought working mothers had on their children.

What we learned was that women consider the things that made them happy or made them feel like they had good families when they were growing up and then they extracted these characteristics from their childhoods, wanting to apply them in their new families. Additionally, their current situations greatly affected their decision-making. In other words, these women's MEs were developed in their childhoods and they brought these hopes, needs, and aspirations into their new family—their WE.

The specific factors, which appeared to be the strongest influences on how women were balancing their ME and WE regarding whether they planned to work for pay or stay at home, were:

♦ **whether their mothers worked,**
♦ **financial need,**
♦ **the "motherhood mandate" (explained below),**
♦ **job satisfaction and,**
♦ **their husbands' support.**

Their Own Mothers

Fifty-five percent of the interviewed mothers had mothers who worked when they were children. When we asked our expectant mothers how they felt about this, they typically responded that they didn't think anything of it at all. It was just the way it was; that's what other mothers were doing too, and in the cases when their mothers worked when they were infants or toddlers, they said they didn't remember. Rare was the respondent who offered, "I suppose it would have been nice for her to be home," and that would only be offered as an after-thought.

While the interviewees agreed that the income was helpful, no one felt it was harmful that their mothers worked. In fact, two of the mothers we interviewed— Zoe and Rosie—said they liked their mothers' working because it increased the family's income. Zoe's mother worked until a younger sibling was born. Once her mom stopped working, Zoe disliked the financial strain of a single income. Similarly, Rosie, a twenty-four year old coed explains, "My mom worked her entire life. I didn't know any different. I don't think I was neglected. The extra income was helpful."

Like Rosie and Zoe, all of the women who were interviewed had a strong tendency to follow in their mothers' footsteps as far as work was concerned. In fact, all of the women who planned to go back to work full or part time had mothers who worked before they were school-aged. Among the three women whose mothers did not work at all, one planned to follow in her mother's footsteps, another will be working full time, and the third planned to run a daycare out of her home. Half of the women whose mothers did not work before their children were school-aged (including Diane) planned to stay at home while their children are infants. Here too it is evident that the women's mothers' role-modeling influenced their own decision making, as the following comments show.

> Lauren: *My mom stayed home, and I enjoyed having her there. Since my mom stayed home with me, that's what I really want to do. That influenced me a lot.*

Vivian, who plans to return to work when her children start school, said:

> *I think it'll be wonderful to stay home and play "little miss housewife" and all that good kind of stuff. My mom returned to work when I started school. I saw mom working as normal.*

Whether their mothers worked or not, 73 percent of the expectant mothers surveyed agreed that mothers should prioritize family over career/work, and 69.8 percent agreed that fathers should prioritize family over career/work. I asked these questions on the survey because I wanted to see if they expected as much out of fathers as they did mothers. As you can see, these women had higher expectations for mothers than for fathers. But I have to admit that I'm surprised that so many DIDN'T think family should be prioritized over work. However, all of those interviewed prioritized their families, so I didn't get a chance to ask the ones who didn't prioritize family why they didn't. Perhaps they simply viewed work as necessary to support families.

While less than 20 percent of those surveyed thought that children suffer from not having a full-time stay-at-home mom, the majority of mothers felt that a mother's employment would have no effect on a child's performance in school, cognitive development, or emotional development (see Table 2 in Chapter 10).

Income

Many women articulated the need for income as their primary motivation to work. All of the women interviewed were currently working, and 19 of the 22 were working full time. Considering the respondents' low median household income ($33,858), it's no surprise that the surveys indicated that two-thirds of the women felt financially pressured to return to work. A blond "call 'em straight" cowgirl named Karen sums up some of the women's feelings: "I cannot afford *not* to go back to work."

Of course, saying that your family needs the money is the socially accepted response for women to give when they justify being in the workforce. They feel less comfortable saying, "Because I want to have a life outside of my kids," or "I feel I really have something to contribute to the world in addition to kids." Our discomfort admitting that work has more rewards than just a paycheck comes from a cultural notion called "the motherhood mandate."

The Motherhood Mandate

All of the women interviewed prioritized their families over their careers. One factor that influenced their decisions was the so-called "motherhood mandate," a position many people hold that women's greatest fulfillment stems directly from being a mother.[13]   This mandate is just "out there" in the culture. Whether you believe it or not, you've heard it. It's in our movies and television shows, espoused by neighbors and relatives and preached from some pulpits.   Just consider this email I received the other day. The subject line read: "The Mommy Test"

> I was out walking with my then 4-year-old-daughter. She picked up something off the ground and started to put it in her mouth. I asked her not to do that.
> "Why?"
> "Because it's been laying outside and is dirty and probably has germs."
> At this point, she looked at me with total admiration and asked, "Wow! How do you know all this stuff?"
> "Uh," I was thinking quickly, " . . . everyone knows this stuff. Um, it's on

```
the Mommy test. You have to know it, or
they don't let you be a Mommy."
    "Oh."
    We walked along in silence for two
or three minutes, but she was evidently
pondering this new information. "I get
it!" she beamed. "Then if you  flunk, you
have to be the Daddy."
    WHEN YOU GET DONE LAUGHING FORWARD
THIS TO ANYONE WHO IS OR MAY EVER BE OR
KNOWS SOMEONE WHO IS A MOMMY.
```

The mothers in my study often brought up the motherhood mandate—either by supporting it or by refuting it. Many of the mothers commented that they did not want to put their children in day care because they felt they would have to miss out on the important moments of the baby's life such as first steps, or first words.   For instance, Nancy decided to delay her career as a teacher, stating:

If I were to die tomorrow, my school work would go on ...Kids would find another teacher . . . life would pretty much continue on, but my family would never be the same. Life at home is really important. That's going to affect my children for the rest of their life. School will be there, but the first few years when they are developing and changing, that's just once. I don't want to miss out on it.

Motherhood is extremely meaningful and important, but Nancy presents some false logic here: That if being a mother is more important than a job, a mother shouldn't work. Of course, she would be of the utmost importance to her children and her children would be most important to her *even if she continued to work.* One comforting finding that sociological and psychological research has repeatedly reported is that working moms do have just as much influence with their kids, and show as much love to their kids, as stay-at-home moms (see Chapter 8 for more on this important topic). There is no evidence to support an idea that stay-at-home moms care more about their children than working moms. And children of working mothers are also devastated when their mothers die.

A second element of the motherhood mandate believes that children suffer if their mothers work for pay. Nancy articulates this belief despite the fact that her own mother worked part-time while her children were young and fulltime once her children were in school. Nancy, like the other mothers, reported no ill effects from her own mother working, but still views working mothers as a social problem.[14]

> *When moms stay home, children have greater self-confidence, know they have family support, and have time with* **family** *(emphasis added). I see kids at school that rarely get any time with their* **parents** *(emphasis added). They crave attention. Children with their* **parents** *(emphasis added) at home have received time and attention, and know they are valued. They have higher self worth.*

By starting with "when moms stay home," Nancy shows she doesn't mean "parents" or "family' when she makes this statement—she means "mothers." In essence, Nancy is vying for a "Female Parent Trump." The Female Parent Trump is a subtle (and sometimes blatant) position that assumes mothers are better parents than fathers. Despite the fact that her language suggests fathers and other family could be substituted, she doesn't really think so. Diane also makes Female Parent Trump remarks when describing why she is quitting her job:

I think it's important to be able to spend as much time as you can with the child while they're young. I feel like that helps to make them better people.

When Diane says "you," she means "mothers." She doesn't think that her husband should be staying home for her child to be a better person. In fact, none of the mothers suggested that a man would be a better father if he didn't work. Imagine applying the same logic of the motherhood mandate to fathers: He has more influence with his kids than he ever will at work. Therefore, he needs to quit his job!

Some women defend against the motherhood mandate by using income as the reason they must work when they actually have other reasons to work. For instance, Angie, who plans to continue working full time, speaks defensively about her decision. She has friends who espouse the motherhood mandate to her. Many of these women's positions are supported or encouraged by their fundamentalist religious values. Angie admits feelings of guilt despite the fact that she doesn't think she's doing the wrong thing. She and her husband have discussed her need to work in order to maintain their standard of living. And Angie derives great job satisfaction from her work.

Lots of my friends say "you can make it on one income if you just would." Maybe they handle finances better.

I want to maintain my lifestyle, and they lay on the guilt. A lot of them are very religious and think that it's very important to be home in the preschool years. I agree with a lot of what they say.

Job Satisfaction

Understandably, women who find their jobs interesting and are rewarded with high status and pay would be less interested in giving up those jobs for full-time motherhood. Similarly, women whose jobs are tedious and with little pay or meaning may look to full-time motherhood as an escape from the bonds of work.[15] The women's satisfaction with their careers influenced their decisions to continue working or not. Vivian, for example, was working two different jobs, both of which she found boring and unfulfilling.

I plan on staying home until my child starts school. I don't have anything against day care. It's good for children because they can interact with other kids . . . I want to stay home so that I can have the opportunity to start my baby off on the right foot and have a bigger influence on the things first.

She looked forward to her child providing meaning and was comfortable with putting work plans on hold. Fallon, on the other hand, really enjoys her job. Even though she states that she'll continue to work in order to have the income, when asked if she'd stay at home if she could afford it, she says no, she'd work anyway. Karen, a fourth grade teacher, also explains that she works because it is rewarding.

*Working with these kids, I know I make a real differ-
ence. Every day I come home real tired but I get to see
them learn, and for some of them, I'm providing about
the most stability they have in their whole lives.*

Husbands

The women not returning to work commonly mentioned tremendous emotional support from their husbands. In an effort to understand more completely how
their work decisions were influenced by their husbands,
women were asked how they would feel if their husbands
wanted them to do the opposite of what they were doing (i.e., work when they wanted to stay home or stay
home when they wanted to work). Respondents often
said they wouldn't have married their husbands if they
had felt that way.

Corinne was one of those women. Career-minded
and happily complemented by her husband's more laid-
back lifestyle, she was surprised by the interviewer's question: "What if your husband wanted you not to work?"

*Oooo, I probably wouldn't have married him. (hearty
laugh) Because I think that, I think that if he's sitting
there saying, "I don't want you to work. I want you to
stay home." I think that would be like a deeper issue. I
mean before the kid even got here, that would have been
an issue. I really don't think that I would have married
somebody who said that.*

Gretchen's situation was the opposite of Corinne's.
She was looking forward to staying home with her infant.
When the interviewer asked, "What if Greg (her hus-
band) wanted you to work?" here's how she responded.

*I guess we would just have to work that out. I mean,
that would be very hard. Hopefully we would have
talked about that, and I would have had some idea of
that before we ever got married and were talking about
having children. So, I don't know, it would be hard.*

These types of responses led our research team to
conclude that the decision whether to work or stay at
home was so important to these women that it was a
point they negotiated in choosing their spouses. "Tall,
dark, handsome, supportive of my desire to work or stay
at home…" – the women appeared to have had a strong
sense of what they wanted to do even before they got
married. And they wouldn't choose a man who would
not be supportive of their choice. Not surprisingly,
couples who agree on important views of the world
and how things should be report being happier and
more satisfied in their marriages. These couples share
hopes, needs, and aspirations, making their WE easier
to achieve.

Also necessary for the ME-WE-ME to be balanced is
for each spouse to have the same amount of time that
they work, whether it be for pay, housework or childcare. Housework, particularly, is an issue related to
marital power because it is unpaid and therefore not as
valued as paid work. It also tends to be monotonous,
and, like your diary, you can never get ahead. Some of
these women shared housework with their husbands
fairly equally, sometimes doing it together on Saturday
mornings. Others had a more traditional division of
labor. How housework is divided is often an indicator of
how housework and childcare will be divided later on.
Couples who are equal are more likely to expect that
situation to continue and, therefore, are more likely to

have equality. Those with traditional relationships before the child often have rather low expectations of paternal participation with domestic work and childcare. Consequently, these families often become even more traditional—with the mothers doing the lion's share of childcare and housework even if they're also working for pay—once the children are born. In these marriages, the ME-WE-ME has gotten out of balance, with the mothers' ME getting lost into the family WE, leaving her with a loss in her sense of self.

The Male Job Trump: An Invisible Wild Card

We live in a time when a majority of women with infants are in the workforce. Of the twenty-two women I interviewed, one woman planned to continue being the sole breadwinner, saying that her husband would be the primary caregiver for their child. But the majority of mothers planned to be dual earners along with their husbands. Of the fourteen dual-earner couples, three women considered themselves the primary breadwinners, three said the breadwinning was equally shared and the remaining eight dual-earning women considered their husbands the primary breadwinners.[16]

Wife Sole Breadwinner	Dual-earner Wife Primary Breadwinner	Equal Earners	Dual-earner Husband Primary Breadwinner	Husband Sole Breadwinner
1	3	3	8	7

Seven women were planning to quit work once their children were born. But, no matter what the couple's employment situation, the tendency was to see the husband's job as more important—in essence, The Male Job Trump. For example, Karen, a high school English teacher who was going to continue to work, considered her husband's coaching job more important than her own. (Surely teaching English is every bit as important as coaching.) The Male Job Trump serves as a type of invisible wild card. No one seems to recognize it, but when it's played, it wins. For instance, no one said "because he's a man" or "because he's the one whose job is supposed to come first." Rather, the gendered reasoning happened below the surface. The conclusions ended up falling along a gendered line, but the women felt that there were actually other factors affecting their reasoning. Consequently, the mothers expected to be the ones doing more of the childcare, even when they made more money than their husbands. Ironically, the mothers tended to think that they would have to make work sacrifices for their family but most thought their careers would not suffer from having families. Unfortunately, work sacrifices do indeed negatively affect careers.[17]

Similarly, all of the mothers were planning to take more parental leave than their spouses. The deference to their husbands' careers was particularly evident in discussions regarding who would take off work when the child was sick. Two-thirds of the women who were returning to work expected to make more of the work sacrifices, doing things like taking off work when their children were sick. Many women seem to think of these tasks as falling to them because of the nature of the work they do. But what I found is that the mothers will justify making more sacrifices no matter what the structure of the job. For instance, Elyse devalued her own job and deferred to her husband's job, saying she would take off because she just had an hourly wage job while Edward's job was professional and salaried. Yet Sarah said she'd be the one to take off *because* she had the salaried job with sick leave. Even when the mothers have careers, they still tend to defer to their husbands' careers. This pattern is illustrated by Fallon and Pam, who claimed their roles as primary breadwinners but still planned to perform a disproportionate amount of the childcare and to make more of the work sacrifices when the children were sick.

Sometimes the reasoning about work sacrifices was attributed to their husband's work environment, saying that people who take time off work for their children are looked down upon by coworkers and supervisors. For example, Angie expressed concern over sharing work sacrifices with her husband by attributing the problem to his work culture. However, in the process she reveals the additional struggle of her husband's attitude:

Work sacrifices will be shared, but not equally because of the inflexibility of his job. Where he works, the men don't take off to take care of sick children. I hope to split time missed from work with my husband, but that battle is yet to be fought. ***He doesn't think he'll know what to do with a sick baby*** *(emphasis added). . . He's flexible; it's his boss that might not be . . . I don't want to be stereotyped as someone who is always getting out of work because of a child.*

Even though Angie is an executive, she views his work culture as less flexible. But perhaps the bigger issue is that of the differing expectations they have for fathers as opposed to mothers. Angie, like most expectant and new mothers, is also anxious about how to take care of a sick baby. The way mothers typically get better at it is through sheer practice. The same is true for fathers.

Of course, there are always exceptions. Corinne is the primary breadwinner in her household and is comfortable naming herself as such.   Her husband is not as career motivated as she is, resulting in a nice complementarity between the two, even with their reversed traditional work roles. In their case, the father is more in danger of losing his ME to the family's WE. Also, we interviewed three couples who worked more as a team, with neither spouse's job taking precedent over the other. With these couples, they truly considered what made the most pragmatic sense in making a living and raising a child.

Housework and Childcare

Another similarity with all of the women interviewed is, no matter whether they planned to work for pay full time, part time or stay at home full time with their children, they all earnestly desired to be good mothers and provide a wonderful family for their children. And the best families are ones where each member's ME is balanced with the family's WE. Two important areas in which the ME-WE-ME needs to be rebalanced when a new baby comes along concern housework and childcare. If one person is doing most of these tasks, she or he may be neglecting her/his own ME in order to take care of the household WE. The women in this study reveal the chasm between intentions and practice in these areas. For example, 76 percent of women surveyed said that, ideally, childcare should be shared equally if both parents work full time, and 82 percent said housework should be shared equally if both are working full time. But later in the same survey, 38 percent of mothers admitted that, if they went back to work after the child was born, most of the housework would be up to them. Obviously, managing a career would be especially hard for these women who may opt out of paid work because of sheer exhaustion.

Two of the women interviewed had husbands who did more than their fair share of the housework, but the majority were doing most of it themselves. Some appeared to be unaware that their husbands weren't sharing equally. Pam, who is the primary breadwinner in a dual-earner couple, puts it this way:

> *He does all the outside stuff and I do mostly in here. I mean, he'll help out. He washes dishes and all that kind of stuff. But he's just exceptional.*

Since "outside stuff," like mowing the lawn, tends to be seasonal, and even at its peak of maintenance is not a daily task, the traditional men's work around the house—yard, cars, home maintenance—only takes about one-fifth the time taken by traditional women's work—cooking and cleaning up meals, laundry, vacuuming, and so forth. Regarding childcare arrangements, two-thirds of the surveyed expectant mothers identified taking care of the child as their responsibility as opposed to their husbands'. Half of the moms revealed that husbands would be minimally involved by using such terms as "*helping out*" and "*when he can.*" Thirty-three percent of the future moms defined their husband's role as something more than minimal. Of course, the childcare arrangements vary according to the work status of the mother. Of the mothers planning to work fulltime, only 23 percent even expected their husbands to share the childcare evenly. If it's not *expected*, it's no wonder that women end up doing more.

For example, Nancy said she and her husband would share childcare, but she would "bear more of the burden." Karen is also returning to work but still feels that she will be doing most of the housework and child-care. Sarah, Wanda and Isabel were the only women interviewed who said housework and childcare would be shared equally. For example, Isabel stated that she would be taking care of the house and baby while her husband is at work, and he will take care of the baby and house while she attends school. Wanda plans to share the childcare and household responsibilities with her husband by scheduling alternate feedings and diaper changing.

Sharing housework and figuring out how to share childcare and paid work are very complex issues expectant parents have to work out. Chapter 3 discusses the transition to parenthood and what the new mothers and fathers didn't expect when they were expecting.

QUESTION TO ASK YOURSELF AND DISCUSS

What and who have influenced you/your wife's decisions about paid work?

Paradise Lost

Chapter 3

What They Didn't Expect When They Were Expecting

In a way similar to how we lose sight of how we actually thought our vacation resort would look when we got there, people's expectations of parenthood get confronted and readjusted over time. One thing all of my interviewees had in common when I re-interviewed them five years into their parenting experience is that—no matter what their expectations were originally—they were proud of their children and glad that they had them. Even though children turn our lives upside down and require us to set them straight again, they also provide immeasurable joy. Some people have more accurate expectations of parenthood because they've been around babies a lot and have "done their homework" by reading about parenthood and talking to other new parents about what it's like. But reality still tends to differ from anticipation.

Interestingly, when asked if their families had turned out the way they had expected, some of the parents said yes—that is until I reminded them of some of the things they had talked about in their first interviews. These parents had simply adjusted their expectations to fit with reality. For instance, Ashley reported that things were as she expected despite the fact that she had intended to work full time and now was not working at all. Then I asked her about something she said in her first interview:

> Interviewer: *You were planning on becoming a medical transcriptionist.*
>
> Ashley laughs: *That didn't work out. You need quiet for that! I didn't even make it through the course.*

What happened to Ashley and others is what happens to us when we go on vacation and actually see our destination. Her mind just re-ordered her memory. She adapted to her situation and so no longer dwelled on those original expectations. However, at the time, dealing with those unmet expectations was stressful. For almost a year, Ashley struggled with different work situations before she finally decided to stay home full time.

Others immediately discussed events that took them by surprise. Many of these events really add on the stress points and, as a result, can throw off the balance of the ME-WE-ME. The largest surprises came in the areas of kids, moves, work-for-pay, the workload at home, bonding, and discipline.

Unplanned Pregnancies

> *Never once in my life have I had sex with the intention of having a child.*
>
> —Father of two

Over half of the couples had at least one surprise child. Even in these times of excellent birth control methods, these couples remind us that they are not foolproof. Fortunately, all but one of the couples has been able to accommodate these children into their marriage. However, Elyse and Edward separated with their first surprise pregnancy. They got back together and had a second surprise pregnancy. Elyse feels that the childcare is completely up to her. She was willing to do that for a while, but as she says, that imbalance has gotten old:

I knew he wouldn't help even before they were born, so I planned on doing it all myself. But it's been five years and I'm tired, tired of having to coax him to pay attention to the kids. We're talking divorce.

Moving

Almost three-quarters of the expectant couples lived in a different house five years later—that's a rate 50 percent greater than the U.S. in general. So, on top of the adjustment of having young children, these couples often are moving to new areas and starting new jobs. All of these changes can be very hard on marriages. In fact, in two cases, the husband lived separately from the wife and newborn for several months. In one case, the couple moved closer to grandparents and in another, the grandparents moved close to the couple. Considerations about moving usually included the loss or gain of being close to the grandparents. In fact, grandmothers were regularly involved in childcare for half of the couples interviewed, providing needed help for these young parents.

Work Changes

Most parents also didn't expect changes with their work, yet two-thirds of the fathers and three-quarters of the mothers changed their work situations at least once in the last five years. Most of these changes were done with the intention of supporting the families one way or another. Mothers tended to change their job situations so that they could spend more time with their families. Usually fathers took jobs that paid better but those jobs sometimes kept them away from their families longer. Five years ago, none of the respondents expected work to interfere with their family lives. This seems like a no-brainer to most parents—of course work interferes with family—but obviously we've forgotten just how much being a parent has changed our thinking. Even as I write this book, I'm very aware of how my work infringes on my family and my family infringes on my work. When these expectant parents were interviewed five years later, they had forged the gap and joined the rest of us parents. Now, the number one complaint of the wives was that their husbands allowed their jobs to interfere with the family. (See Chapter 4 and Chapter 8 for more on the conflicts paid work creates.)

Domestic Work

Additionally, couples hadn't anticipated just how overwhelming the whole "having kids" package is.

Bridget: *I knew it would be different. I didn't know how different. I told somebody, I said, 'Having is kids is like work.' The days go by really, really slow*

> *sometimes. And you think, 'Oh my gosh, we're never gonna get anywhere.' You know, the kids drive you crazy and, 'Oh, if I could, if I was just away for a little while.' Then all of a sudden one day you look up and think, 'My goodness, look how big he is. Look how tall she's gotten.' It's just like you don't recognize it while it's going on.*

While housework had been manageable before children, now it is pervasive and never ending.

Interviewer: *Has the way you split housework changed since before you had kids?*

Angie: *Yeah, I guess it has because before, I pretty much did everything and now everything just doesn't get done. I think he does more and I do less (because of childcare) but it doesn't equal what we were doing before we had kids. Our house is never straight anymore. I think back to before we had kids and just how straight and how clean everything was . . . and even with him helping me when he can we just let a lot of things go.*

While housework didn't cause conflict before, now it does. Moms particularly are noticing that "he's sitting watching TV while I'm mopping toddler spills in the kitchen." Often one person's perspective on housework matters is quite different from the spouse's. Take Tim and Terri as an example. During Tim's interview he said:

> *She gets all upset because I didn't get the laundry folded. All right! I should fold the laundry.*

Apparently, laundry was discussed before I arrived because when I interviewed Terri an hour later, she brought up laundry too, even though no questions referred to it:

When he's watching the kids, he won't do anything else. He won't even get the laundry started.

Terri and Tim have three children. Just one child tends to be an adjustment for people and two really throws them off balance. Of course, those with three are now outnumbered! With three children, Isabel describes how even the good times can be a challenge:

Well, the stress of having more kids, especially. It's much more demanding, and, I don't know, they each vie for your attention, either one. So we try to balance each other. If Jennifer is needing cuddle time, inevitably Jason is going to want cuddle time, so usually Ike ends up sitting in the chair with all of them in his lap. Or one of them will come to me and two to him. But it has been a challenge as far as learning that kind of stuff.

Sleep Deprivation

The parents of three are also the ones still accommodating an infant in the house, which leads to another of their underestimated expectations: Sleep deprivation. Couples knew they wouldn't be getting as much sleep but living the reality of that for months on end cuts into your performance during the day. Bridget describes the adjustment:

It's hard. The first year that I worked and I had the long drive, and had to get up early, I slept during lunch. I literally, I took two pillows and a blanket to my job and at lunch I slept on the floor. Because, I, couldn't do it. I couldn't get enough, I couldn't get enough sleep being here and being there and everything.

Mothers of three have been dealing with sleep deprivation for years. And it's a problem even when you're a stay-at-home mom.

Terri: I'd fall asleep! Right here in the living room while I have two preschoolers to watch! That's not good!

Sleep deprivation is reduced when the couple shares the nighttime duties. Isabel recalls that as she describes her struggle now that her husband, Ike, is stationed in Afghanistan:

A lot (of sleep deprivation) since he's been gone. When he was home it wasn't as bad. We were equally sleep deprived, 'cause he would, even though I got up to feed Jennifer when he was working, he would get her up and change her and we would have a conversation or whatever. He just felt bad if he wasn't helping, but since he's been gone, I see why it's so important to have two parents in the home.

Nursing

Another surprise for some mothers was the difficulty in breastfeeding. There's so much propaganda about how wonderful breastfeeding is for both baby and mother that most mothers expect this to be a tremendously satisfying experience. Some mothers, however, find the experience distressing and oppressive. For one thing, nursing is very time consuming. Babies sometimes want to eat every two to two-and-a-half hours and often take thirty to forty-five minutes to feed. Consequently, mothers may only have an hour-and-a-half in between feedings. Diapering, laundry, and other maintenance quickly take up that time. In short, it can be difficult to have a life outside of breastfeeding.

When asked what advice she had for new parents, Olivia addresses breastfeeding:

> *Nursing, it's not easy. These books make it sound like it's just so easy, you just latch the baby on and you're just fine. No! It's not easy. You talk to 90 percent of the people, it's difficult, I mean, it's hard work! Yes it's natural, but it's hard work, getting your baby to latch on and take. You just have to be patient and work through it and know that if you can make it past pretty much the first two months, you're fine. There's just that period that you're just gonna be like, kind of frantic and just tired. And emotions, your emotions are changing, your hormones are getting back in balance. Just know that there is a light at the end of the tunnel and that it's so worth it.*

Conspiracy of Silence

Olivia's feeling of not knowing the huge difficulty she was getting into with breastfeeding is but one part of a more general cultural problem people face: They aren't told how difficult being a new parent really is. They hear all of the wonderful stories about how happy people were when their children were born and they listen endlessly as friends and coworkers brag on their children. On top of that, friends and family—especially potential grandparents—are pressuring them to have children, telling them how great it is.

But many people's experience is that it's not all that wonderful there at the beginning and they wonder if they have made some huge mistake. "There were days that I wanted to get in my car and drive out (U.S. Highway) 377 and never come back!" exclaims Corinne as she reflects back on those first months. Parents also wonder why they don't love it as much as everyone else seems to. As David, a very involved father of twin infants, confessed: "I feel like I have a new hobby that takes all of my time and all of my money and I don't even like it."

But such admissions are seldom made in public and if they are, they may receive harsh rebukes like, "Oh, they are just so precious." And "my children are the most important things in my life."

It's not that David and Corinne don't love their children, it's that they didn't know how much their lives were going to be turned upside down and they're thinking that they are unusual. Bridget and Lance are two more examples of parents who had trouble bonding with their new baby. "I was never around kids, ever," Bridget explains, reflecting on her unplanned pregnancy. "When I had my baby, I had never bathed a baby, never fed a baby, never changed a baby, nothing. I'd never put a diaper on, and so I was terrified, you know."

With ample experience with nieces and nephews, Larry stepped up to the plate and did a majority of the nurturing during those first weeks as Bridget got the hang of it.

Similarly, Laurie took over during Lance's difficulties which he describes below:

Yeah, I mean that was a shock to my system. I'd never been around kids and all of a sudden I've got this little baby that I'm responsible for, and I'm thinking, I can't do this, and you know I came around to it, after, after a while... I wanna tell you, seriously, I disappeared for six months. I would find any excuse I could not to be here. I'm not happy about it, believe me, I wish I could have been here to see everything happen. I missed a lot of stuff, but, all you can do is learn from mistakes. When John came along I kind of figured most of my feelings out. It was a pretty rough time, I tell ya.

Five years later, Lance still finds excuses not to be at home. Despite Laurie's continued pleas, he sacrifices the WE of his family for the ME of his fishing. Since Lance is doing something enjoyable while Laurie is home with the baby, he seems more acutely aware of his abandonment of his home responsibilities. They go more unnoticed by fathers like Jerry, Adam, and Oscar, who voluntarily spend excessive time at work.

For many, the commitment to being an involved parent precedes the bonding. Mothers tend to do this as a matter of course since our culture so strongly teaches that mom needs to be 100-percent involved. Some mothers and fathers see this as "coming naturally" to mothers (which contributes to guilt feelings for mothers when it doesn't). Janice views it this way:

I feel like I am closer emotionally. Maybe that's just because, I would say I'm the mom and I gave birth to them. So, I have this extreme attachment to them . . . I think if not now, at some point our love for them will probably be just as equal because obviously they're more . . . the kids to the mother. We're more attached to kids. I think it's really just kind of natural attachment for obvious reasons.

But most gave credit to the amount of time being spent with the child as the primary reason for the strong attachments.

Terri: *I'm a lot closer because I'm with them a lot more.*
Lance: *Laurie's closer because she's with them 24/7.*
Brandon: *I was closer with the first one because I was doing most of the childcare. But now, it's her 'cause she spends more time with them.*

Nancy builds on the importance of time for bonding by describing how she and Norm solved a problem:

There was a time when Josh was really attached to me and I think at that point we kinda talked and realized he needed more time with Norm. And even though it was hard at first 'cause Josh kinda fought that and resisted it at first, the change was what made them so much closer.

Drawing on the "coming naturally to mothers" notion, Jerry continues not to put in the time required to have a strong emotional bond with his children:

She's closer . . . She's a female. She has more emotional feelings around kids since she carried them and brought them into the world.

Interviewer: *Could it have anything to do with the extra time she spends with them?*
Jerry: *Not that. As a male, I'm not as emotional.*

But whether or not they think women are naturally more connected to the children, most fathers recognize the need to put in quantity as well as quality time with their children to develop a strong bond. Norm planned to be an involved dad from the start. Even though he would be working full time and his wife, Nancy, was going to stay at home, Norm had a strong commitment to "giving Nancy a break." And true to form, Norm did what he said he would do even though he didn't immediately feel a strong emotional connection to his son, Josh. The emotional connection came when Josh was two and had a life-threatening accident while Norm was caring for him alone. It was several hours before Nancy could join them at the hospital, and it was during this time alone with his son, with the threat of losing him, that Norm fully realized just how deeply he loved Josh.

Norm was one of the few parents who articulated how being a parent actually has gone better than expected:

> *Bringing a child into your family is an adjustment, but I think it's been a little better than I even expected. Just because, I don't know, I guess I had some preconceived notions that it was just going to be 100 percent different. And it is different in some ways, but I feel like in a lot of other ways some things are still the same.*

Corinne also describes how being a parent has gotten better with time:

> *I think the first six months was just a blur and a negotiation with yourself, with your husband, with your baby, of, 'How does all this work? How does all that fit together?' People do it all the time, you know. And so, I think that's the hard part, people do it all the time, it happens all the time. But, are we doing it well? Who pays the price for the short comings?*
>
> *I'm not a baby person. Like the, 'Ooh, aah' thing. And so I like my relationship with James much more now than I*

did then. I think for some people, it's just the opposite. They like the whole baby part, and then this gets in the way. Well, now he's a person, and we can have conversations and that kind of stuff.

Having twins, however, overwhelmed Deborah:

I think I had expectations of being able to do it all—being supermom and I'm not. And that's something I still struggle with—not being able to keep up with things . . . I thought it would be easier. . . It's very difficult.

When I had the twins, I didn't want to be by myself with them. I guess I was afraid of them. With John (her third, who came two-and-a-half years later), I could relax and hold him and I enjoyed that.

Deborah's husband, David, stepped in and did the lion's share of nurturing with his infants while Deborah learned to adjust. The difference with David compared to the other fathers who did close to an equal share of parenting when their children were under three is that he has *continued* to do half the parenting for his three children.

Super-Bonding

In a very different way, Terri and Janice were surprised in those early months. They didn't expect that they would want to spend all of their time with their new baby.

Terri: *I expected to retain all of who I was before I had her, and a lot of that independent, free, and wild me is gone, not because it had to be but because I chose to do it.*

Terri had a successful career and intended to continue working full time while her mother cared for Linda. But she found being separated from her baby unbearable. Her mom suggested she give it a couple of weeks to get used to it and Terri complied. But after the two weeks were up, she gave her two-week notice. For Terri, however, this has not been a permanent situation. Over the last five years, she's worked full time, part time, stayed at home full time and is now going to school full time. She loves being a mother but also enjoys a life beyond mothering.

> Interviewer: *Do you enjoy your school?*
> Terri: *(with "Valley Girl" irony in her voice) Yeah, like, I get to talk to adults!*

On the other hand, Janice intended to stay at home all along but it was more because that was what her husband, Jerry, and his family wanted: "I didn't expect to fall completely in love with my baby." She adds with a chuckle, "I'd look over at Jerry and say, 'Who are you?'"

Now pregnant with her fourth child, Janice only plans to work during her children's school hours. She tries to spend every one of her children's waking hours with them and she fears the emptiness she might have to face as they grow up. Janice is notably the exception with her complete commitment to her children and one has to wonder if her lack of a ME might have detrimental effects for both her and her children down the road. For one thing, not having a ME can cause mothers to get their ego needs met through other people and the other people many parents use are their kids, which may put undo pressure on them.

Conflict over Parenting

None of my couples anticipated having conflict over parenting before their children were born. All of them admit some conflict now. On a scale of one to ten, most rated the conflict about a three or four. The chief topic of the conflict was differences in how they disciplined their children.

Most of the couples had communicated with each other about their concerns.

Nancy: *We have varying styles, and that probably has been a little bit of a challenge in that we have to adjust to doing things with different styles. But I think that that's been good 'cause then I see how his style benefits Josh, and how my style benefits Josh. I can tend to be sometimes a little more relaxed with Josh, and he's a lot more consistent, which encourages me to be more consistent . . . There's a time when you can back off a little and relax. So I think we balance each other out.*

Some of the time one parent would defer to the other as the better disciplinarian and truly seek to be more like him/her. But more often, couples were at an impasse and relatively accepting of the fact that their differences would continue. Janice and Jerry are an example:

Janice: *Spanking. Sometimes it's hard for me because she is so strong-willed, that it doesn't work for her; it's like "whatever." I think Jerry's still pretty firm on it, but sometimes I'm like, "Oh, yeah, I don't know." So that's probably our main thing (conflict)*

> *. . . I think it's just a matter of finding out what works . . . what works for him doesn't work for me.*

Appropriately providing discipline for our young children requires a lot of time and a well thought out game plan. Chapter 8, "Every Home Is a Home School," addresses this important topic in more detail.

In the marriages that seemed to be the most stressed (including the divorced and separating couples), conflicts over discipline figured prominently. In all of these most stressed-out cases, mothers were frustrated that the fathers were not providing discipline because of how little they were seeing their children; and when they did, they didn't put boundaries on their kids' behavior. Indeed, these mothers were dealing with dashed expectations.

The Big Picture regarding Marital Satisfaction

The couples in my study reflect a national trend when it comes to marital satisfaction. While marriage has a generally positive effect on women and men, parenthood often causes a reduction in how satisfied spouses feel about their marriages.[18] Much of the effect children have on the marriage depends on factors such as the age of the spouses and how solid the marriage is before they have kids. Marriages that have a well-established balance between their MEs and their WE do not have the precipitous drop in marital satisfaction that other couples report. The following chapters discuss how to have a solid marriage but first let's explore typical trends in marital satisfaction over the course of a marriage. Sociologists routinely ask people on surveys, "How satisfied are you with your marriage?" while also asking for age, gender, and length of marriage. The rest of this chapter reports on the consensus of those studies.

Marriage is good for people. Numerous studies have reported that married people are healthier than single people, they report being happier than singles, and married men have less stress than single men.[19] Both men's and women's marital satisfaction scores are extremely high—often the highest they ever will be—on their wedding day. This fact probably doesn't surprise anyone. Weddings are hugely important events! Just think about how people change their plans, buy gifts and incur other considerable expenses to be present at the weddings of family and friends. And they should! The fact that every culture on the planet has wedding ceremonies—a time when people drop their plans to celebrate the coming together of two lives—reflects the significance of this ritual. People won't come together like this again for the bride and groom until their funerals, and they're going to miss that one!

So, this is it, THE day that people come together to celebrate these individuals. It's no surprise that people start their marriage with extremely high marital satisfaction. Women usually report higher marital satisfaction on the wedding day. We think of the wedding day being more her day than his. She's the one who has been encouraged to think about it more ever since she was a little girl, with toys and games, and by friends and family. And she, likely, has done more of the hard work planning the wedding, not to mention the fact that the ceremony focuses on her! I recently went to my friends' wedding, which can serve as a typical example. When Aaron, the groom, walked in with his groomsmen, the music was the same as it had been while the congregation waited for the ceremony to start. He and his friends were dressed almost identically in black tuxes but Aaron's ascot was white. Then the music got better and the flower girls came in, followed by the bridesmaids in dresses deliberately designed to make the bride look better. Then the music got louder, we all stood and turned around and there she was! The bride, tada!

In early marriage, too, women report higher marital satisfaction than men. Much of these differences in scores have to do with adjusting to marriage (even if they cohabited first—marriage is different) in terms of freedom and communication. In both cases, women have spent their lives in a manner more similar to marriage than men have. Consider the notion of freedom: It's men we think of losing their freedom. "That ol' ball and chain" refers to wives, not husbands, simply because women have never had that kind of freedom in the first place. I can illustrate the difference through examples of calling my students' apartments. When I call a female student and ask, "Is Cally there?" her roommate can tell me if she's there or not and when she's expected home. If she wants to, she could probably tell me where Cally is. Also, if Cally doesn't come home or report in that night, her roommate will worry about her.

When I call the apartment of a male student and ask, "Is Justin there?" I've heard the roommate say, "Just a minute, I'll check." To a woman, this sounds funny—the idea that you don't even know if someone is in your apartment or not. In fact, I've been in the living room of a house shared by four guys before, with three of them in the living room with me. The fourth came home and walked through the living room and down the hall without saying a word. In a house with four women, the other roommates would have been following her down the hall, saying, "What's wrong?"

Women have many years of practice in terms of letting people know where they are, worrying and caring for one another and sharing their feelings. These elements are essential skills for a successful marriage, the building of their WE. Men know this and that's why they're willing to learn this new way of living. It partially explains why married men are healthier, happier and have lower suicide rates than single men. But it can be an adjustment for them just the same. Sometimes women are not very empathetic about the fact that the men are learning a new way to be in relationship.

The Bad News

Before I tell you the bad news, remember that married people—both husbands and wives—report being healthier and happier than singles. That said, on average, both men's and women's marital satisfaction drops precipitously with the birth of the first child. At this point, wives' marital satisfaction becomes lower than husbands' for the rest of the marriage. It's also at this point where women, more than men, report not having enough time to themselves (their ME). Marital satisfaction continues to drop for both spouses until the youngest child leaves home, with the lowest point being when the children are adolescents. Like I said earlier, how much of a drop depends a lot on how well the couple was doing before they had a child, but generally there is a drop and childfree marriages typically do not report as much of a drop.

All of this doesn't mean that the couple is dissatisfied with their marriage; it just means they aren't as satisfied as they once were. One reason is because the attention is now focused on the child(ren) rather than just on each other. This also explains the drop at adolescence when the issues related to the children become more complex. Additionally money and time become scarcer when a couple has children which can cause the spouses to be in competition with each other, trying to get enough for themselves. When the children leave home, couples can readjust their roles as parents back to spouses. "Mom" looks across the breakfast table and says, "Hi, I'm Mary" and "Dad" says, "I'm Bill." Most parents are glad that they had children, feeling that the good far outweighs the stressors they cause and couples that operate as a parent team weather the difficulties better than those who compete against each other.

IMPROVING MARITAL SATISFACTION

One study of veterans from Iraq found that those who spent 15 minutes a day writing in a private journal increased both their and their spouses' marital satisfaction.[20]

The unexpected realities discussed in this chapter make up a lot of the reason couples need to rebalance their lives and relationship—their ME-WE-ME—once the children come along. The next chapter explores the ins and outs of the transition to parenting and the rebalancing of the ME-WE-ME.

QUESTIONS TO ASK YOURSELF AND DISCUSS

What did/do you expect before you had/have children regarding housework, childcare and paid work? How will you share tasks like caring for your sick child or night feedings with your spouse?

Chapter 4

Adding Players to Your Team

Rebalancing the ME-WE-ME

As discussed in the book's introduction, couples need to find a balance between their needs for independence and autonomy (ME) with their needs for closeness and relationship with their spouse (WE). Each of us has our own set of hopes, needs, and aspirations, and each of our needs includes the need to belong. Our relationship is a balancing act between these needs for togetherness and our need for space—especially since some of us need more space and some of us need more togetherness!

Adam describes how he and his wife, Angie, actually work together to nurture each other's MEs:

> *I supported her with her work on her master's degree and then once she got out of school, she supported me on getting my master's. I think we've always been that way. I mean as far as being supportive. We try to attain not only our family goals, but also our individual goals.*

Hopefully couples have developed this sense of balance before the first child comes along, because now there is another person to consider—a person who will have a relationship with each parent, as well as a new person in the couple's WE.

Of course, the couples keep their first WEs as well. Those in my study were particularly aware of their needs for time together as a family and most also were aware of their needs for space. And, like most parents of young children, their time together as a couple was the most neglected.

Paid work is a major avenue to meet a person's individual ME, providing space from the other members of his/her family. Work can be an opportunity for an individual to achieve and be successful. As described in Chapter 6, work can be a very good thing, not only providing needed money, but also helping individuals mature and feel like they are making a contribution to society. Since most work requires us to be away from home (and even when it doesn't, it requires that we direct our attention away from our family), work can impede the family's WE. While a couple may have been well-balanced before the new baby, that balance often becomes an issue once again. Now, all at once, we need more money, but we also need to be spending more time at home because there is a new relationship to develop in addition to maintaining the original one.

A major area of stress for many couples comes right here, with wives thinking the husbands are allowing their work to interfere with family time and the husbands feeling like they have no choice.

For example, Wanda feels like Willie prioritizes his work over his family. But addressing the same issue, Willie says:

*Balancing family with work is very hard . . . Even though I
know I do stuff at work, I kind of put family ahead and then
wind up paying for it down the road.*

Sarah also feels like her husband, Sid, allows work to
encroach on family time:

*He works with a supervisor that sometimes we don't agree
with her views or her ways. And I think whenever we discuss
that, it kind of affects us sometimes. Because he's trying to
tell me his hands are tied and stuff, and I'm saying, 'Well,
why don't you do this?' Or, 'Say this.' Or, 'Why don't you ask
her for a policy?'*

Sid actually took his job in expectation of becoming
a father and definitely feels torn between the money he
earns and the cost of the time away from family:

*With my job, it's an ongoing battle. I'm working so much
I'm not even taking care of my own family, at times. It's
a double edged sword. I think everybody within my work
that has children definitely deals with that problem. And it
definitely comes up a lot, with people at work. You know,
'How can I take care of others when I can't even take care
of my own?' You're up at work and your child is sick at
home. You need to be at home. It's hard. It's very difficult.
As far as what they can do, I think my job is as flexible
as it can get.*

It's clear that he's aware of Sarah's complaint that he
needs to tell his boss, "No," too:

*You do have to stand up, you know. Like yesterday, working
a sixteen-hour day. . . I'll get paid for that, but I won't get*

to make up for the time (with my family). The time's lost. It's gone. But I get paid for the time.

Adam thinks that Angie is supportive of the demands his job puts on the family while conceding, "I could do a better job planning." But Angie's support has its limits:

He could leave his cell phone at home when we go on vacation. But he doesn't and they call and call.

The flip side of the issue of one spouse working too much (always the father in this study) is the other spouse winds up doing more than her share of the childcare. Not only does this tend to impede the mother's own need for ME, it neglects the father's need to develop a relationship more fully with his child. Both Diane and Elyse describe taking on too much of the child nurturing and care when their first children were infants. Diane learned her lesson and corrected with the second child:

Things that I did wrong with Andrea . . . always doing everything for her instead of trying to split it up whenever he was home. I would just, anytime she cried, I would always run to her and I got her so used to that, I think, that whenever he tried to do anything she didn't want anything to do with him. She would always call for me. That wore me out.

Diane's problem is typical of stay-at-home moms. They tend to feel like taking care of the baby is their job, and since they are with the baby more, they develop ways of soothing the baby that the fathers haven't developed. So, rather than giving the time to the father to develop his own methods, she just takes over, often feeling like she's the only one who can do it right.

But, as I mentioned, Diane learned her lesson and Derek was much more involved with the second child's care from the start. Yet even five years later, Andrea continues to be closer to her mother, as Diane describes:

> *I think in the very beginning you have to try to work that out and figure out. At first, he could probably give her a bath and be fine. But she was a much more demanding child as far as always wanting me. It seems different now with the second one, we just kind of automatically split it up. I didn't always try to do it all.*

Even though Elyse was working full time, she assumed that her husband would not be willing to be involved with childcare because he wasn't involved with the children from his first marriage. Therefore, she resolved to do it all herself. By the time she realized it was too much for her, the die was cast. She is constantly trying to get Edward to spend time with their daughters, but he won't. In retrospect, Elyse wishes she had handled the situation differently. She offers this advice for expectant parents:

> *Be realistic [about] relationships, or your particular relationship with your spouse. Figure out what the problems are now and be aware of them, because I think that if you are aware and realistic and know what you need to work on before, it's not so hard when you're put in the situation. Because it's life-changing. I know for me, it turned my life completely upside down trying to learn how to adjust with having to take care of someone else who couldn't do it.*

When men like Edward neglect the house and kids, women like Elyse are much more likely to consider divorce.[21]   For Elyse and Edward, the ME and WE are so off balance that divorce is indeed in their plans. There is very little WE between Elyse and Edward—they aren't sharing the same vision for their family. The only WE is between Elyse and her kids. Her chief complaint is that Edward isn't involved enough with the children. But, sadly, the WE that so much needs to develop between Edward and the kids is likely to disintegrate after the divorce since he will no longer be living in the same household with them.

ME Time – Put on Your Own Mask First

Most of us don't listen anymore when we ride on airplanes. We casually flip through magazines or talk to the person next to us as the flight attendant goes through the emergency procedures. But let me remind you of one of the things the flight attendant says: If the cabin loses pressure, oxygen masks will drop down from the ceiling. Put on your own mask first and then help your child. They anticipate the fact that we parents would naturally seek to save our children first so they are making a very pragmatic point: If we're passed out, we're not going to be able to help our children. If we only focus on our children, we, in essence, have too much WE, which ultimately hampers the children. Our children need us to be healthy in our own right, with our own needs being fulfilled through channels other than them. When we have no life outside of our children, it can be stultifying for them as well.

At home with three children under five years old, Terri gets right to the point with her chief complaint:

Not enough me time. Not enough help . . . There's never enough arms to do everything that needs to be done.

And her husband knows it's a problem too:

I really think that our relationship affects me at work, because I worry. I'll call home and see how she's doing and say, 'Hey I love you, what's going on, are you okay?' And if I don't, I just feel guilty because I don't.

Fortunately, Terri and Tim are addressing this very real need Terri has. She's getting it fulfilled to a great degree by going back to college. Tim's mother is providing a wonderful aid to their family functioning by watching the children while Terri attends class and studies.

Leisurely activities also contribute to ME time and may be as simple as getting away for a break. I was surprised by the number of times Wal-Mart came up in the interviews. Forty percent of women answered "going to Wal-Mart" when asked how they go about getting a break. But I don't think going to Wal-Mart is adequate ME time. Having used Wal-Mart as a break myself, I know I always ended up doing some shopping for the family while I was there. Similarly, scrapbooking is a WE activity even when people get away from the kids to do it. Laurie reveals just how little true ME time she has when she describes her leisure activities:

I've started scrapbooking, and I've got friends who do their books, and so, yeah, we'll go and do that. I go to my moms' group . . . still, I take the kids, but that's done on my own time.

Laurie's husband, Lance, does a better job with ME time—he goes fishing, a popular leisure activity among

the dads I interviewed. Illustrating just how difficult getting a good balance is, the problem for full time workers
like Lance is that leisurely ME time is in direct competition with WE time with their families. Laurie is frustrated with Lance for not spending more time with his kids.
There's no magic formula for the perfect amount of
time parents should spend with their children, but one
recent study found that fathers spend as little as twelve
minutes a day in direct interaction with their children.
Work is the major siphon of parent time. Sixty percent
of the mothers I interviewed said their top complaint
was that their husbands spent too much time working—
time that needed to be given to their families. A third
of the women, including Laurie, were unhappy about
their husband's leisure activities that robbed time from
their families. Whether it's the need to reduce work
hours or deny themselves some leisure activities, fathers
like Lance need to find more room for their children.[22]

Both Lance and Jerry claim that they try to offer
their wives time for their own ME's, but both of the
wives decline. The women claim they decline because
what they want is to all be together, nurturing the family WE. The result is the husbands just take that time for
their own leisure.

> Janice: *He offers. He suggests I go out and do something
> with friends, but I don't want to. I want us to all
> be here together as a family.*
> Laurie: *He thinks it will all get evened out if I take time
> away too. But the kids need time with us both
> here.*

While it's understandable that the mothers want
to have family time all together, given that the current

set-up isn't working, they would do well to accept their husband's offer and take time for themselves, nurturing their own ME and allowing the kids to get some extra daddy time.

Because men and women have grown up in a society that puts more pressure on fathers to be breadwinners and more pressure on mothers to be nurturers, full-time working mothers typically realize they will have to compromise ME time in order to have enough time in direct interaction with their kids. Many mothers have added breadwinning to their responsibilities but still feel responsible for childcare. Mothers typically spend three times as much time in direct interaction with their children as fathers, and, on average, the mothers perform 65 to 80 percent of all of the childcare.[23] As one of these dual-earner couples, Adam and Angie feel guilty about the number of hours their children spend in school or with a babysitter (usually forty hours a week) so they are reluctant to go out, just the two of them. But Angie notes that guilt doesn't keep Adam at home, thus creating an imbalance of leisurely ME time in their marriage:

> *But it never fails if certain people call and invite him to play golf or to go hunting, he's all too willing to jump and go. And I don't mind that as long as turnabout is fair play. But when one of my friends calls and wants to do something, it never fails that he's really tired . . . I don't take those day-long times away to relax and I would like more of those because I am tired and tense.*

Adam, however, is slow to admit that he has more free time. He starts by saying "It depends on what you call free time." But he finishes with:

> *I probably get away more . . . If I try to take off, to play golf or whatever, I try to take from vacation time at work. That way I know I'm not drawing away pretty much from the family.*

Adam overlooks the fact that taking vacation time for golf is not only taking away from work time, but also taking away from time he could be spending with his family on vacation. Angie, on the other hand, denies herself a housekeeper:

> *All of that money that would go to a maid, if you add it up for a year, could pay for most of a vacation.*

Fathers like Derek Johnson also are compromising their leisure time in order to spend it with their families. As the sole breadwinner, Derek spends his time after work and on the weekends doing half of the childcare. He is very happy and comfortable with his commitment of involvement. But when asked if he'd like to have more children, he responds:

> *No, because we, I feel like . . . Diane and I feel that an additional child would be beyond our comfort level of the balance that we have between the time we are able to spend at work and together, and with the two kids that we have.*

Derek's response is typical of involved dads: When they put in the time required for childcare, they are less likely to want more children. This in no way means they don't love the ones they have—in fact, they're more involved with their kids than the typical dad. That's what makes them more realistic about the costs (time, social and emotional) of having more children.

In the Johnson family, it's Diane who has the ME time. Her children are in Mother's Day Out for five hours a day, two days a week. No doubt much of this time is devoted to errands, but Diane also regularly meets with her friends. Similarly, Olivia is a stay-at-home mom whose two children are in Mother's Day Out two days a week. Olivia gets much of her ME needs for accomplishment met through charity work. Her ME time also includes regular bimonthly nights out with her friends. Sometimes stay-at-home moms feel guilty for taking time for themselves like this. But it's healthy and good for them. When they take good care of themselves, they're taking care of their children's mother— and that's good for the kids.

Corinne describes how ME time is much different for divorced parents:

I think being divorced is a double-edged sword because on one hand, you have all these issues. But then the only perk, if you could even call it that, is that when Christopher has James, I have time to myself that I know as a full-time wife and mother, [you're] not gonna get. 'Cause there's that weekend where James is gone. As a wife and mom you get those breaks, but it's never in your own house. It's like you have to go away to get it. You don't ever get to be in your house by yourself.

For a long time, I would cry every weekend that James was gone because it just broke my heart. So that part of it has kind of been an interesting kind of negotiation within myself about how can I utilize this time. But I think I get what I want with kinda the save-and- spend method. I save up for what I know that I need, whether it's time to myself or whether it's a new pair of shoes, and then I spend it. So, it's a constant kind of an ebb and a flow. 'Cause if there's thirty-one days in a month, I might get to be me, or have me, by myself, for a day out of that. And so, you just kind of really learn to value that time.

Divorced parents with custody of their children obviously have a huge challenge finding ME time while meeting their children's needs. Corinne has figured out a way to negotiate this dilemma effectively. For her, as she begins to date, and for the rest of the couples I interviewed, another challenge is finding time for each other.

Time as a Couple

Nurturing the marital relationship WE is perhaps the biggest challenge for parents of young children. The kids require constant attention and, on top of that, work demands our time. There just doesn't seem to be enough time for mom and dad simply to be wife and husband.

"When we get to fighting, I'm like, 'Wow, we need a date!'" Like Nancy, most of the people I interviewed were familiar with the idea that they should have a "date night" regularly but no one mentioned actually doing this—not regularly. It's not because they didn't want to, it's because a date night requires they be away from their children and at least one of the parents typically already needed to be devoting more time to the kids.

A second limitation is finding a babysitter. "What we probably don't do enough is we don't get away ourselves much because we're real picky about who keeps the kids," explains Adam. Olivia and Oscar are lucky in this regard. Oscar's parents live only a few miles away and Olivia's are only about an hour away. With this extra cushion of family care, they were recently able to take a vacation together—just the two of them. Not only could they afford the (free) childcare, they didn't have to feel (all that) guilty since the kids were getting time with the grandparents and vice versa.

Because of willing grandparents, Sid and Sarah have been able to take a trip together every year:

We need to be together as, as husband and wife, and have that time. It doesn't have to be for a whole week.

For those not quite as lucky as these couples, one way to get some couple time together is after the kids go to bed. Use the time to talk or play cards or some other activity (other than watching the tube) around the house. The dishes can wait.

Nancy: *Now that Josh is around, we tend to get our time together after he's gone to bed.*

The Extended WE: Grandparents

Grandparents—especially grandmothers—figured prominently in these young families. There were four instances where the grandmothers took over childcare so their daughters (and in one case, daughter-in-law) could work. In three other families, daughters and their newborns lived with their parents while the new fathers established themselves in a new job in another town. Indeed, almost half of the couples intentionally lived close to the grandparents and in all but one of these cases, the grandparents babysat regularly. These families consider the grandparents' proximity very seriously when they consider moving. In addition to babysitting,

47% of parents mentioned their mothers and fathers as role models for their own parenting. And 27% reported receiving praise for their parenting from their own parents. Indeed, grandparents are playing an active role in helping these couples rebalance their ME-WE-ME.

One family in this study, however, had entered the phase of life called "the sandwich generation." Courtney's parents are in poor health, requiring both Courtney's and Caleb's attention to be split between caring for their young children and their aging parents. While they willingly give their time and energies in both directions, this couple is particularly challenged with the need to balance ME and WE.

Even with the considerable challenges of maintaining a balanced ME-WE-ME in our modern, busy lives, most of the families I interviewed were succeeding. The next chapter describes the common characteristics of the highest functioning families.

QUESTIONS TO ASK YOURSELF AND DISCUSS

How might Laurie and Lance resolve their imbalance in their ME-WE-ME?
Can you apply Jesus's admonition to love your neighbor as yourself (Mark 12:31) to their situation?

Chapter 5

Winning Teams

What Makes the Most Successful Families

The floor, you could've eaten off of it. And now, it's like you could still eat off the floor but it's because there's so much food on it. There's Pop Tart crumbs. I mean, you could make a meal of what's on the floor.

—Frank

I look at the floor in Frank and Fallon's home. It's completely clean. I'd eat off it, but I'd have to supply my own food. A major adjustment to parenthood for obsessively tidy Frank is the messiness of kids. But Fallon and he work together, sharing paid work, housework, and childcare equally. Of all the couples I interviewed, Frank was the only father who was truly doing half of the childcare—and maybe a little bit more.

The families where dads were highly involved in the care and nurturance of their children were the most highly functioning. These couples didn't share any particular structure of how they split paid work. Some couples had both partners working full time, some had the father working full time and the mother part time and some had her home full time. But generally the best families were those that had figured out how to balance the ME-WE-ME. They made sure both adults got time together with each other, time as a family, and time to themselves.

Balancing the WE: Sharing Common Hopes and Dreams

One common characteristic of the most successful families was that the parents shared common hopes and goals. Clearly, an important part of what helps young families achieve their hopes and goals is by having both parents involved in daily childcare. When the father wasn't involved (with my couples, the mother was always involved), the family wasn't as happy. This involvement was motivated intrinsically within each parent—it wasn't something they were forced into doing. They did it because they wanted to, and even when they didn't feel like it, they still felt obligated. Roughly 30 percent of my sample shared this characteristic, with the fathers believing in the hands-on perspective of fathering from the start and being equally or near-equally involved in the daily interactions with the children. All of the mothers in this study were doing at least 45 percent of the child care. That, no doubt is a wonderful thing for kids and moms. But when moms are doing most of the care, they tend to get stressed. We've all read the bumper sticker: "If Momma ain't happy, ain't nobody happy." The reason is clear to most of us: Moms tend to be the emotional heart of the family. They also tend to be the practical heart of the family. They are the ones most likely to know everyone's schedules, not to mention everyone's shoe size. So, if she's not happy, that sadness reverberates to every person in the family. (Of course, when Papa ain't happy, ain't nobody happy either. This is especially true of the involved dads.)

Moms tend to be happier and more satisfied with their marriage when dads are deeply involved in the daily care and maintenance of the kids[24]. Moreover, studies have shown that moms are happier in their marriages and family life when they merely *perceive* that the father is a good helper. But as we saw earlier, sometimes mothers have rather low expectations of their husband's involvement. When men actually perform a good amount of the childcare, the results are even more positive. Everyone wins when dad (along with mom) is involved with the kids. Moms get a break, dads get to know their kids better, and kids get the benefit of two involved parents rather than just one. For instance, children score higher on school tests when fathers are involved with their care.[25]

Years ago—in the 1970s—it occurred to people to start making fathers feel more a part of the birthing process. That movement has been enormously successful, with almost all married fathers participating in it. Truly, fathers feel more a part of their own children's lives than they did before they were included in the labor rooms. Leaning back on two legs of his chair, with a big smile, Sid talks about his efforts to bond with each of his newborns:

> *Experiencing the birth and all that coming out, and cutting the umbilical cord—I was right there. I was the first one to hold them and all that, bathe them . . . But for me, I felt I had nine months to catch up on. Being tied emotionally in. There was a lot of stuff that we did. I read different books*

of a father's role . . . to the point of having sympathy pains (laughs). I played music on her stomach. And I'd lay my head on her and talk to them when they were in the womb. So, I really felt that he really knew my voice. Well, both of them. I think that's what happened with both. They came out, they got that breath of air. They're crying, they're upset, you know, 'I'm not where I'm supposed to be,' and all this. And I start talking to them and they calmed down. So that was a wonderful experience with both—being tied to them.

Fathers can build on that momentum and increase their levels of involvement both before and after the baby is born. Increasing their involvement increases their own enjoyment of (and emotional investment in) their children. During pregnancy, they can be a part of the parenting team by giving up caffeine, alcohol, and tobacco right along with their wives. Sometimes people act like there's no need for the expectant father to make these changes, but the mother of his child needs his support. Anyone who's been on a diet knows it's easier if the whole household participates. Making dietary changes is a way the man can ease her load and truly empathize with one of the sacrifices of motherhood. Men need to be supportive—even when she says he doesn't have to. If she can do it, he can too. And when he does it too, it makes life easier for her.

After the baby arrives, many men have learned what it means to step up to the plate and help with those difficult night feedings. Sleep deprivation is a serious issue (see chapters 3 and 9), but the solution isn't to put it all on mom. Sometimes moms actually think it is okay for them to handle the night feedings because "he has to get up and go to work in the morning." But the one who is taking care of a newborn (often with a toddler

who needs care, too) also needs rest. Some fathers—
like Adam—are sympathetic to the cause. They get up
and do the out-of-bed work like bringing the baby to the
breastfeeding mother and doing the diapering. Adam's
wife, Angie, brags on her husband: "From the start,
Adam would get Katie out of bed, change her diaper,
and bring her to me to breastfeed."

Frank, the fastidious father quoted at the beginning
of this chapter, talks about how there was no option
with twins. "Yeah, we each would have a baby to feed
at night," he recalled. If you don't have twins, another
option is to alternate nights to ensure each of you gets
a good night's rest every other night. Lastly, if you can
afford it, hiring someone to come in and do those night
feedings can make your life go much easier, particularly
if you have multiple births.

Norm, a rotund biologist for a research lab, recognized that merely doing half the diapering when he was
home from work wasn't nearly enough for him to claim
that he was doing half the parenting since his wife was
staying home full time. Even before Josh was born, Norm
planned to give Nancy a break when he came home. He
stayed true to his intentions and tried to change all of
the diapers when he was around because she was changing them all when he wasn't. This intentional involvement results in Nancy's having "no complaints." Nancy,
who began working part time at a childcare center when
Josh was three, reports:

> *When Norm comes in at night he helps quite a bit. He will
> take over some and give me a little bit of a break, especially if
> I've been doing it all day long. So, it is nice because it gives
> me a chance to re-energize and to get ready to do it again.
> 'Cause to really be consistent in parenting, it takes a lot of*

energy. And so it's nice when someone else can come in and you kinda take turns.

When describing how Frank and she divide child-care responsibilities in a typical day, Fallon, who works full time as a loan officer, reflects with a smile, "Sounds like he does a lot, doesn't it?" That's because Frank is truly doing half of the childcare. His involvement comes from a commitment to his wife, his kids, and a desire to be different from his own father who didn't share in childrearing. One way Frank is involved with his kids is to include them when he runs errands.

> *See, my dad wasn't the 50-50 dad when it came to parenting. Now he was 50-50 dad when it came to things around the house. He always helped my mom with laundry, with cooking, things like that. But as far as the kids, the kid thing was mom's deal. He kinda did his thing and I wasn't always a part of that . . . I wish he had spent more time with me. So I knew before we had kids . . . I'm gonna take my kids with me when I go somewhere. They're gonna go to Home Depot with me, and they're gonna go to wherever, and I pretty much load them up and take them with me wherever I go.*

Sid discusses how his involvement with the family is a bit out of the norm in his conservative community. But as a committed Christian, he sees his active fathering as a way to be the family man he's called to be:

> *I don't mind doing that (a large portion of the housework) because it's just part of how we're set up. I get flack for it a lot, sometimes from my friends. Just because I do a lot of the housework and stuff. And I do the yard work too. But she's always with the kids. Those are areas where I work more*

often than she does. I have longer hours, I'm called out at unexpected times and that's just where I see something as my part as the husband and as a father to help out in the matter, you have a responsibility. You want to make your marriage work, you wanna be a father. And that's why I think that it's important that the kids, the boys, especially the boys, that they see me doing these things. And that they want to help me. The oldest one, he's wanting to help out, now, so he sees me starting to clean and he wants to clean. And the other one, he's starting to do some stuff like that too. Just mocking stuff, but it's important.

What Sid realizes from his own experiences has been supported in research. Positive results from kids helping dad with housework include:

- **Having more friends at school**
- **Obeying teachers**
- **Having less anxiety in young boys and more "warmth" in young girls**
- **Being less likely to suffer from depression or being socially withdrawn**[26]

For the most part, the mothers in this study were delighted to have their husbands take an active role in the parenting. But Corinne, a professional journalist, describes a reality mothers need to face when they're lucky enough to have a mate who takes an active role in parenting: He may do things differently from how she would have!

James was about three months old. You know how babies get, like where they lay, they get that little bald spot on the back of their head. Well, Christopher didn't like that. So he buzzed it. Took the clippers, and buzzed off, because James was born with a lot of hair. And so he buzzed off every bit of hair, like down to just baby fuzz. So he called and told me at work, 'Hey, guess what I just did?' and I'm like, 'What?' And he's like, 'I just buzzed James's hair.' And I'm like, 'O – kaaay.' And I remember, I consciously said, 'Okay, he did that while I was at work, that was his decision.' And then of course we laughed about it. I mean it was bad. It took him forever for his hair to grow back after that. I was like, 'O my gosh…' [Shaking head] I went in the bathroom and I cried. But I didn't say anything to him about it.

Balancing the "ME":   Each Adult has Goals and Interests Outside of the Family

Having a sense of identity and a strong sense of self (ME) are necessary ingredients a person brings into a loving relationship. We each have our own sets of hopes, needs, and aspirations and those are part of what makes our relationships healthy —we do "have a life." That makes us more interesting and less needy. This ME can get lost when people first become parents. Mothers are particularly at risk of losing their ME in order to take care of the family WE. Whether you think it's biological or the result of the tremendous expectations other people put on mothers—either way—they often need to learn to feel okay about taking time for themselves and continuing to "have a life" beyond taking care of their children. Terri describes this struggle to preserve both partners' MEs in her marriage:

His need to be independent and my need to be independent while still being together . . . it's hard to do that when you're with the kids because, you know, it's a total self-sacrifice.

For Terri this struggle is worsened by the fact that Tim doesn't help enough, in her estimation. But her mother-in-law has helped by taking care of the kids while she goes to school.

Tim gets a lot of his ME needs satisfied through his job. Work is one way women and men continue to have goals and interests outside the family, with the added benefit of providing income for the family. In my study, the couples who had two people working or going to college were more likely to have both members of the couple happy. Karen, a blond mother of two who has worked as a high school English teacher for eight years, describes her work satisfaction:

> *I think, the type of person I am, I need interaction and I need a purpose. Not that staying home is not, there is a purpose to that. But I just think, for me, that I need to be making a difference, not only in the life of my child, but in the world too.*

Nancy, too, comments on going back to work, saying, "One of the nice things about work is I get time away from Josh and that makes me a better parent."

Leisure activities are another way people can take care of their ME. "We both take our time off," says Fallon, describing how she and Frank take care of each other by providing time for leisure activities. "We need some off time away from the kids or whatever. We say, 'Take it,' you know, 'I'll stay home with the kids and you go do your own thing.' And he does the same thing for me."

Norm describes how he and Nancy also make the effort to support each other's time with friends:

I feel like Nancy and I are both pretty good. If there's a day that I want to go out and go fishing or whatever with some friends, then she always lets me. I mean, short of us maybe having previous plans or something. And I try to do the same for her. If she just needs even just a couple hours to go alone and shop or a day with some of her girlfriends, then I'm more than willing to do whatever I have to do to let her do that. So I feel like we trade off. If one time I go, then within several days after that I'll try to let her do it.

However, when it came to leisure, some of the stay-at-home women were guilty of tending to the family WE rather than to having a life of their own. When I asked questions about leisure time, an amazingly high percentage of them listed shopping at Wal-Mart (and one, Target) as leisure activities. Since going to Wal-Mart usually involves buying groceries, diapers, and other home and family items, this activity is at least partially family work even if you go alone. So while going to Wal-Mart can be a break from childcare, it doesn't nurture an individual's life beyond children.

Some stay-at-home moms had their ME satisfied through their involvement in volunteering or activities with friends. For instance, Olivia meets with friends to go bowling twice a month and has busied herself with volunteer work—and not all of that is wrapped up in her kids. Diane also meets regularly for an evening meal with friends. These times that stay-at-home moms leave the kids with their fathers also provides nice opportunities for father-child bonding.

No One Is Overstressed

Young families in our culture tend to be stressed. It takes a lot of money to fund our lifestyles and work demands a lot of our time. Building a career is very demanding and usually takes place when our children are young and require a lot of our time and attention (birth to five years of age). But three families in this study were doing a particularly excellent job of handling these stressful years. These parents worked together as a team, nurturing each other's MEs and the family WE as described above.

Research has found that women are more prone to depression and physical illness when they are overly burdened with housework and childcare.[27] The most stressed-out people were two stay-at-home moms, Laurie and Wanda. Laurie is home by choice but Wanda had to quit working because of health problems. Both women feel stressed because they are responsible for their children virtually all of the time. Both complain strongly that their husbands aren't there enough. Both husbands know this but don't do anything to change the situation. So while communication is important, it's not enough. For both of these women, a part time job could help them get some ME interests going. Even if their salary went entirely to paying for childcare, it would be worth it because pursuing an interest besides kids, home, and family could relieve some of their stress, which ultimately would make everyone in the family happier. Chapter 8 provides more details on how to make real changes in unhappy situations.

Living Within Their Financial Means

Enjoying a new four-bedroom house on two acres of land, Karen reflects on a time when she and Ken could hardly get by:

> *At first, when we first got married I just had a little 20-hour job at the college. He was working at the Western Sizzlin'*

restaurant and so we actually rolled quarters for rent at points. But the whole experience brought us closer together. We never take anything we have for granted.

When families lived within their financial means, they were less likely to be stressed. When they were in college, Karen learned from Ken to count pennies. She identified then that he was good with money and followed his lead. Most of the couples who were good with their money were like Karen. They learned to live within their small financial means early on and continued to be cost-conscious even as their incomes grew. Now Karen credits their new house to those habits she's shared with her husband since college.

Other couples experienced changes in their financial situations that caused a burden. For instance, 56 percent of the couples who went from having two incomes to only having one had significant struggles with making ends meet. Most of the remaining couples had husbands who had very high incomes. The Walkers were the only couple who have been successful with living on a modest income. No doubt part of their success was due to the fact that they only had one child. People have a tendency to underestimate how much children cost, if they think about it at all. However, current estimates of what it costs to raise a middle-class child to age 18 (before college) are $231,470.[28] When you figure in the amount of lost wages parents incur, the figure jumps significantly since it's common for at least one parent to reduce paid work hours because of the need to increase time parenting.

Of the four most financially stressed families, one— The Tankersleys—had three children and the other three families had two. The Tankersleys tried many different constellations of work and childcare arrangements. The best arrangement so far was for Isabel to work and Ike to stay with the kids. With a college education, Isabel is able to earn more money in fewer hours than Ike. Adding to the rationality of this arrangement, according to Isabel, Ike is the more nurturing parent. But both Ike and Isabel have traditional notions of how gender roles should be, so they've chosen to have Isabel at home while Ike works months at a time away from home. Consequently, the family now has two major stressors: Not enough money and not having Dad around as much.

Two of the financially stressed families with two kids—the McLaughlins and the Gibsons—described wanting a third child, even after a long interview during which they described how stressed out they were. With only one income and no "wiggle room" financially, Laurie McLaughlin will need to return to the workforce in order to support another child. The Gibsons pull in a good income—around $60,000 a year—but they've made poor financial decisions, including buying cars that they couldn't afford and commuting a combined total of six hours a day, which leaves their family with very little time and a whole lot of stress. They will need to undergo major financial planning and significant lifestyle changes in order to bring a third child into a healthy family situation.

The Mythical Re-creation of the "Traditional Family"

Many Americans idealize the notion of the "traditional family," thinking of it as a worthy example for their families to follow now. We often imagine these families as they existed in the 1950s. In this depiction,

Dad worked for pay and Mom stayed at home with the kids. These days people still describe the traditional family as having two kids—probably because of *Leave it to Beaver* and *Ozzie and Harriet*—when in fact the actual number was closer to four. And the misperceptions continue from there: Only the white middle and upper-classes could afford this arrangement, and even then, it required that children share bedrooms and the family shared one car. (See Chapter 7 for more about how the media have shaped our perceptions about our work and family lives.)

The family structure of the men as the sole bread-winner and the woman as the full-time housewife and mother peaked in 1960, when 40 percent of American households fit into this traditional mold. But this period of American history also had serious social problems. Factors that contributed to keeping white males' salaries high made life difficult for others. For instance, Americans these days tend to overlook the sexism that kept women at home, unable to find jobs with good salaries and restricted from owning property. Similarly, racism kept minority wages low. As Stephanie Coontz explains it, we remember what's good and forget what's bad.[29] Let's also remember that the 1950s and '60s gave rise to bestselling books like *The Organization Man* and *The Lonely Crowd,* both of which addressed the mindless conformity people felt they were expected to adhere to at work and in general. This is also the time when Betty Friedan drew an enormous audience with *The Feminine Mystique* in which she challenged popular notions such as housework being an expression of femininity.

Another way we typically stray from an accurate recollection of the historical 1950s family is that we've added our own flourishes of what we think the ideal family looks like—and we don't all agree on what those things are. With the couples I interviewed, about 20 percent re-created the notion of the traditional family, particularly in terms of wealth and father involvement. They think of themselves as holding traditional family values but their notions are far from historical reality and, I would argue, far from ideal because of the reduced presence of Dad in the household. Jerry and Janice, for instance, report that people praise them for the way they are managing their family lives. Janice stays at home with their three children (and they hope to have more.) Jerry works as a rehabilitation therapist about 70 hours a week. Like a third of the fathers interviewed, Jerry leaves before his children awaken and returns home in time to tuck them into bed. Since he is only home for 15 to 30 minutes be-fore bed and he has three children, he's only averaging about 5 to 10 minutes a day per child. Of course, this average will only get worse when they have another baby. To further complicate matters, Jerry plans to change jobs and expects he will have to work more hours. He sees it as a wonderful career opportunity and justifies the additional hours, saying it's better for him to put in the time now so that he can be more available when the children are older. Here, Jerry represents a fairly com-mon sentiment among fathers: They discount their own value to their children while their children are young.

When I interviewed Jerry, I reminded him of some-thing he had said in his first interview, when his wife was expecting their first child:

Interviewer: *You mentioned that perhaps you would start working less hours than you were before Carolyn was born. Have you been able to do that?*

Jerry: *No, no, because...I'm very driven as a business person and wanting to succeed as much as possible. I still wanted to get to that point...the reason I haven't backed off on hours as far as work is because...they're so young. I figured if there's a time for me to work as much as I can, it's when they're young. And as they get older, they become more interactive. Then I'll want to start taking off.*

Men like Jerry are saying this even while their wives are continually encouraging them to spend time with their children. And the children typically crowd around and fight for time with Dad when he's there. Why do these fathers not realize how important they are?

One reason could be their strong identity as bread-winners—that making money is the most important thing they do as fathers and husbands. But it doesn't completely explain Jerry and Oscar. Both men have jobs that would allow them to work fewer hours. They are both making over $100,000 a year, twice the national median, which brings us to reasons two and three—self-entitlement and materialism. These men are driven to make more and more money no matter what time sacrifices their children have to make. Apparently, they're doing it because they love their work and they love the prestige they get from making money, having nice houses, cars, and other high-dollar items. Here is where their wives appear to be willing colluders. Janice and Olivia brag about their husband's success. They give their husband privileges, such as time to watch TV or play video games, while they continue to work mopping floors and cleaning kitchens. They also allow their husbands more leisure time to engage in various hobbies in the evenings or on the weekends. Actually, "allow" is not a word either woman used. Jerry and Janice joked about how Jerry would ask but then go ahead and leave even on the rare occasions when Janice said, "No." Olivia framed it as "just the way Oscar is." But even while expressing desires that their husbands spend more time with their families, Olivia and Janice explain that this is just the consequence of getting to stay at home—to having the "traditional family."

But, of course, these aren't the traditional families of the 1950s and '60s.[30] Typically, fathers in those families worked forty-hour weeks. When asked why they had the work-family split that they had, Olivia put it this way:

Probably because . . . I always knew that my mother was there for me no matter what. Not to say that a working mother is not always there for their kids, but I just want my kids to know when they are young that no matter what, I am going to be here for them . . . And I know on a day-to-day basis that I'm just a very affectionate person to my children; I want them to know that they're loved and I think that is the most important thing you can teach a child is to know that they are loved and that—no matter what—their parents are there for them.

Interviewer: *Did you feel like your father was there for you?*

Olivia: *Yes, but those were different times. He came home for lunch and then he was home at 5:00.*

Olivia doesn't see the irony in her statements—that she could know that her father was there for her even though he worked, and that her own kids are not getting that knowledge about their father whom they rarely see.

The real trade for Olivia is not trading Daddy time for a traditional family because in the traditional family, Daddy was around a lot more than Oscar. Instead, they've traded Daddy time for a lavish standard of living. On face value, this seems okay with Olivia. She's getting what she wants: A nice house, time with her children, and time to invest in civic activities and hobbies. Oscar seems to be getting what he wants too: His career, his hobby, and someone to take care of all of the childcare and housework. Certainly, Oscar and Olivia have a nice life and their children are well cared for. But their choices seem to suggest they don't know the wonderful benefits that the whole family enjoys with a father who is active in child nurturing and care.

Sometimes people like Oscar and Olivia feel like there are no options besides working long hours; that employers make these demands and if we don't conform, we'll lose our jobs. The difficult task of juggling work demands with family needs is discussed in the next chapter.

QUESTIONS TO ASK YOURSELF AND DISCUSS

What do you think of when you hear the term "traditional family values"?

How well does your family handle money??

No Man or Woman
Is an Island

Chapter 6

Competing Demands

Work and Family

Vincent, an angular, bespectacled man, leans back in his easy chair which is aligned for perfect viewing of his big screen TV. Beaming with pride, he boasts, "I make a lot of money." Throughout our interview, Vincent makes these kinds of assertions, reflecting his strong identification with being a breadwinner. For Vincent and most of the men in my study, being a good breadwinner is seminally important to their feeling like they are good fathers—even to feeling like they are good men.

Vincent's remarks come with a sense of relief. As a construction worker, making "a lot of money" hasn't come easy for him. "For a while there, I was working three jobs." In addition to his fulltime job with the county, he clerked at a convenience store and cooked at Sonic. Understandably, this young father was stretched beyond his limits. Landing a well-paying job two hours from home provided only a slight reduction in work hours, however, once his 20-24 hour commute per week is factored in. (The US average commute is just over 4 hours per week.) But even while describing his long hours, Vincent adds, "I feel real good when I get a big paycheck."

Vincent's wife, Vivian, also works full time and together they embody a phenomenon called the "middle class slide." The "middle class slide" describes the way that families are having to put in more and more hours to maintain the same standard of living as middle class families had in the 1950s and 60s.

The average American worker clocks in 100 more hours a year than she or he did in 1980[31]. It's only an extra two hours a week, but after you do it for a year, you've put in more than two extra weeks of work that year. And to what end? Often we are not given a choice on this matter. The American workplace expects us to work more and more and the culture supports it. If given the opportunity to work fewer hours for less pay, many people say they can't afford to. Sometimes this is because of low wages. Other times, people can't afford to work fewer hours because of earlier poor financial decision-making. Consequently they find themselves in debt.

Other families work long hours because they don't want to give up the nice material things that come from that extra income—everything from $10 tubs of popcorn at the movies to cars with seats you can heat and cool. Parents in my study were often aware of this reality. Sarah and Fallon provide examples of the work hours vs. material goods dilemma. Both have professional jobs and both talked about wanting nice stuff for their kids. But in both of their cases, there was no easy solution to reducing their or their husbands' work loads.

Yes, they wanted nice things but their fulltime, professional jobs wouldn't have allowed them to reduce their hours by two per week even if they asked. Alternatives to these good jobs are rare. In most cases, American jobs require full time work in order to receive benefits, and part time work ends up paying considerably less per hour.

This chapter explores the American work culture and the effects it has on individual families and the members of those families.

More Than a Paycheck

We need to work. Most people readily acknowledge that. Having the household income that white, middle-class men provided in the 1950s and 60s now usually requires two workers. We immediately recognize our economic need to work but the couples I've interviewed also admit their desire to work. When I asked if they would want to work even if they had enough money and didn't have to, most people said, "yes." They recognize that work is more than a paycheck. Sigmund Freud said that to love and to work was what most characterized what it meant to be an adult. It hits a core of meaning and purpose deep within us. Work helps us contribute monetarily to our families, but it also can give us feelings of contributing to the greater society, a notion Karl Marx identified as crucial to people. Both men and women identify the good feelings of accomplishment and independence that work provides. They talk of feelings of fulfillment and contributing to society as well as noting that they made a lot of friends at work. Indeed, many people said they'd "go crazy" after staying at home for a while.

Besides the economic, social and emotional needs it fulfills, work can also help with the relational needs in our marriages and families. People need togetherness (the WE) but they also need space (ME). The structure of work helps us to achieve that ME—that identity separate from our other family members. After being a stay-at-home mom, Nancy recognized this need to have a life beyond that of wife and mother. She and other mothers attest to how work helps them to be better parents because it gives them a break from the children and a chance to face new challenges.

Yet, while people agree we need to work, many feel we're working too much. Indeed the young parents in this study often mentioned that time at work was keeping them or their spouses from having needed time with the children. Vivian describes the predicament of many:

> *If I could work halftime and be more of a mother than I can be right now because of the time crunch, and if it wouldn't put my family in a financial bind, I would do that. I enjoy having the time away from the kids. I need that, but I don't like not having any time. That's hard.*

It's one of life's unhappy ironies that the time in our lives when work requires the most of us (early in our careers, when we're having to learn the fineries of our jobs and having to prove ourselves to others) is also the time when our families require the most of us (when our children are young.) These parents are greatly affected by the work demands in our culture, whether they want to be or not.

How American Culture Influences Us

In order to identify values in a culture, sociologists look at how people spend their time and note the underlying meanings of what people say. Sociologists note that our culture values activity and work despite complaints otherwise. This focus on work is certainly apparent in typical practices in the workplace:

- **Entry level positions often start with only zero to two weeks paid vacation per year (as compared to six weeks in Europe).**
- **The new professional will often work 50 hours a week or more.**
- **Fathers are unlikely to take paternal leave even when companies offer it.**
- **We're pushed to work, work, work.**

You can also tell how we value activity by how we tell (or even complain to) others about how busy we are. For instance, think about this typical exchange:

"How are you?"

"Oh, you wouldn't believe, between work and Cody's piano and Jessica's soccer, I'm surprised I don't meet myself coming and going . . ."

That's so much more a common response than,

"Great! Haven't done anything all week."

I was at about this point in my Introduction to Sociology class one day when a student blurted out, "*I* don't value that! I don't want to work all the time!"

I feel her pain.

Interestingly, many in the class did not. They have been shaped by the culture they grew up in, to the point that they too value work over most things, including family. That's because our culture is so pervasive; it's all around us. Most of us don't even notice it. We're shaped by values in our culture, and we accept them without giving them serious thought.

Unfortunately, even if we as individuals don't value what our culture does, we're affected by it—especially with a value like work. When we do think about it and decide to go against the norms of our society, we usually feel pressured to go with the flow. My husband and I have both chosen to control how much we work so that we can have more time with our family, even though it means less money for us. Doesn't that sound like a good thing? Many people think so. But they also tend to not understand. Both of us have turned down opportunities for advancement because they would require us to work more hours, causing us to have fewer hours with our children. People expect that workers will take promotions when offered, no matter the time costs.

It's understandable how parents can have trouble saying "no" at the workplace. Many employers view a preference for caring for family members as lack of commitment to the job. Also, when parents are offered the option of a few hours more away from their families in order to make more money for those families, it can be hard to turn down! It's not just the money that is enticing. As Hochschild found in a major study of Fortune 500 corporations, both fathers and mothers would use paid work as an escape from the work of taking care of their children.[32]

In order to understand how American families have gotten between the rock of workplace demands and the hard place of family demands, we can consider history. Before the Industrial Revolution, American families typically made a living either by farming or through "cottage" industry, where products like furniture or clothing were made at home. Children were usually around their parents and participated in the family labor. With the Industrial Revolution, factories required workers to leave home to do their jobs. "Good" jobs were designed with the idea that the worker would make a "family wage" which would free his wife to do the cooking for him, cleaning for him, raising his kids, tending to his emotional needs and replenishing him for another day's work. These "family wage" jobs were only available to white men, consequently discriminating against women and minorities. Even though we think of the traditional family as containing a male sole breadwinner, a female who does unpaid domestic labor full time, and their children, this has never been the norm. According to the US Census Bureau, only 40 percent of American households were comprised of these "traditional families" at its peak (1960). Now it's more like 7 percent.

Even though the economy has changed to where few families have someone home fulltime with the kids, our work structure continues to be largely unresponsive to the needs of families other than providing income. The machine of the American economy whirs out of control, with productivity being the bottom line, requiring more and more of workers with little or no regard for the fact that the workers have families. What little attention employers pay to families comes wrapped in the package of attracting the best workers to their businesses so that they can be more productive. American business and politics may give lip service to saying families are important but the structure of our work paints a different picture. Families are expected to prioritize work over family, conforming the needs of their children or other loved ones around the needs of the workplace. Families are also expected to move should an employer need the worker elsewhere.

Being well socialized into a culture that expects families to conform to the workplace, the parents I interviewed were unimaginative when it came to ways their jobs could accommodate their families. Like most Americans, they're accustomed to figuring out how their families could accommodate their jobs. Diane, a stay-at-home mom, was typical of the respondents. When I asked how her husband's job could be more supportive of the family, she said, "It could pay him more." And when I asked Mike how *family* affected his *work* life, he responded, "There are activities the kids just can't do because of my schedule," which actually answers the question of how his *work* affected his *family*.

His Work; Her Work

All of us, men and women, develop our identities through interactions with others. We all need social networks to help us identify who we are and to support us as we face the day to day complexities of life. Men particularly derive notions of themselves through the social contexts of their work. As noted in chapter two, a man's primary identity tends to be as a worker. He is his work. Even when men become fathers, they typically keep worker as their primary identity, interpreting what it means to be a good father as being a good breadwinner. Men are much more likely to prioritize work over family—to the point that they might see their work aspirations as a way they help their family. The logical consequence here is that to be a good family man you would actually need to be away from your family. Of course, breadwinning is absolutely important—"Gotta eat" isn't just an expression. For good reasons and not-so-good, fathering turns out to be an extension of working—a new reason to work longer and harder.

Consequently, any goals for fathers to become more involved caregivers will require changes in the workplace. These changes are slow in coming and have been mostly the result of more women/mothers in the workplace. For instance, we now have paternity leave available in many corporations, the result of extending the concept of maternity leave to fathers. However, even when paternity leave is offered, most men don't take it. The leave they take with the births of their children is usually in the form of vacation or sick leave. Part of the reason for this is because paternity and other family leave may not be paid, which is a huge problem facing American workers and is addressed later in this chapter. Another reason is that men are often afraid to take paternity leave, fearing others will think they're not being committed to their job. Especially if the norm is for men at a particular place not to take paternity leave, other men are afraid to be the first. Mothers who want their husbands to take more time off after the birth of a child, or want their husbands to take their equal share of sick days when the baby is sick, need to be aware of the strong influence the work culture has on these men, and fathers who want these things have to consider the work context as well.

The work culture is more than just what policies a corporation offers. More important is what family friendly practices people actually use. If a business offers flextime but no one takes it, one must think that something is going on in that work culture that prevents people from doing it. Corporations that are rated "family friendly" need to be rated not only by the policies present but by the number of employees taking advantage of the policy.

Women tend to be more willing to take chances at work. They're more willing to put their jobs on the line for their children than men are. Yet before women get too haughty (thinking that they are the real cowboys; the ones standing up for what needs to be done), we must remember that the greater culture puts more pressure on women to be responsible for the children. So, just as cultural influences keep a man from taking paternity leave (for fear that other men won't see him as manly, or fear that he'll lose status at work), a woman feels responsibility to take maternity leave. People will see her as doing the right thing when she does. Unfortunately there is ample evidence supporting the fact that women lose status and pay for putting their families first, the burden of family comes first for many of them—even when they need the money.[33] While a woman does pay the price of lower wages and status for putting family first, the stereotype that says women should put their family before their jobs also gives a woman license to quit a job she doesn't like in order to stay at home with a newborn. A man is likely to feel pressured to do just the opposite; to keep a job he hates *because* he's now a dad.

He Says/She Says

The fact that women and men receive different cultural pressures (she is to be the caregiver, he is to be the breadwinner) often causes a basis for disagreements in marriage. As an example, consider the Carter family. Willie and Wanda met while Wanda was still in high school. As a senior, she started working at a department store where Willie worked as a low level manager. Shortly after her graduation, they married and Willie was transferred to a new store several states from home. Seven years and two kids later, a combination of Wanda's poor health, Willie's demanding job and the lack of family support programs in their area are bringing this family to crisis. Forced to take a demotion because of health issues, Wanda decided her wages were too low to make it worthwhile after paying childcare. The result is that she is home fulltime with the children, seldom getting a break. Making the situation worse, Willie often leaves before the children (ages 3 and 5) get up and comes home after they are in bed. Willie works 60-70 hours a week. He says he has to; she says he allows work to encroach on their family. On his one day off a week (sometimes it's just a half day off), he wants to spoil them. This leads to another conflict: Discipline. The kids misbehave enough that Wanda doesn't like going out to restaurants with them. She ends up being the "bad cop" parent and Willie won't toe the line. Consequently, the kids feel closer emotionally to their father than their mother, and go to him when they need comforting.

Worse yet, the Carters live in a rural area that doesn't offer programs such as Mother's Day Out. Recurringly through her interview, Wanda discusses the themes of enjoying work, her husband works too much, her kids are driving her crazy and she stopped work because it didn't pay well enough to make it worth her time. Sometimes people on the outside can see solutions better than those caught right in the middle of them. In the Carter's case, perhaps some of the family tension could be alleviated if Wanda got a job. Even if she didn't make any more money beyond what she would have to spend on childcare, she could get a break from the kids—and, let's face it, they could get a break from her! Getting some time away would improve her outlook. She would get to talk to adults and get some time away in order to appreciate her children. Again, the time away would help the kids appreciate her too!

Willie and Wanda's disagreement over Willie's work is not unique. Several other couples described the same problem. Mary says Mike lets his work interfere with his ability to help with childcare. "On his day to pick them up from daycare, it never fails that he's late. Something always comes up." Sarah says the same about Sid, except she frames it more in terms of how Sid allows his supervisor to take advantage of him while Wanda and Mary frame it more in terms of their husband's choice. Mary and Sarah are fulltime workers and have drawn strong boundaries around their work, reducing the amount it interferes with their family life. Their experience makes it clear to them that it is possible for their husbands to do the same. Their husbands feel a responsibility to their work that the wives don't understand. The husbands view their breadwinning as essential to the family. On top of that, they think it would be irresponsible for them to let their employers down, reflecting a notion of, "Real men aren't slackers at their jobs." Underlying this perspective for many men is the desire to make themselves

> **RESOLVING DIFFERENCES**
>
> When spouses discuss work and family with each other, they need to consider the powerful influence gender socialization has had over each of us. After hearing your spouse's perspective, repeat it in your own words before offering your perspective. Doing so will help you understand each other better.

indispensable at work which increases their job security. Having and keeping a good job is key to their feeling like they're good family men. They point to how essential their salaries are to their family (even when their wives make as much or more). A real man isn't going to let down his family by not making as much money as he can.

Outdated Attitudes are Getting Us Down

There was a time when parents worked near or in the home and school was more accommodating of work. Our schools were designed around working parents and working children: Children were out of school for planting and then again in the summer for crop tending and the harvest. Schools are still accommodating farm families but less than three percent of our families are farm families. Schools need to accommodate the type of working families we have now and the workplace needs to accommodate families as well.

Not only are outmoded work and school schedules failing the needs of American families, traditional gender roles are too. Females are socialized to think they are more responsible for the kids (and they also reap more of the rewards that come from involvement with the kids). I'll call this the motherhood mandate because our culture mandates mothers to be the most responsible parent. The career mandate applies primarily for men, where they feel most responsible for their family's income. Women are in the workforce but are much more likely to think about caring for children when considering a career: For example, women are more likely to consider being a teacher so that they have the same hours as their children and are off work in the summer.

Having women be the ones primarily in charge of the children causes them harm economically, and since our culture equates money and power so much, it ends up giving them less power and prestige in the culture overall. Consequently, women end up doing more housework and having less free time. A vicious circle is completed when they and their spouses decide the woman should make more work sacrifices to take care of the children since they aren't paid as much.

Social commentator Rhona Mahony suggests that, for the above reasons, there will not be gender equality in our society until men are doing half of the childcare. Of course some men do half the childcare for their children. But by far the norm is for women to do most of the childcare for their and others' children. Men aren't doing half the childcare because, 1) on the whole they can trust that women will do it, so they are freed from having to, 2) women, on the whole, don't trust men to do an adequate job with the care and 3) men have been brought up with the career mandate—they're not doing what they are supposed to do to be good fathers and even to be good men unless they are in the workforce working however many hours and doing whatever needs to be done to "succeed."

Just as having a rigid motherhood mandate disadvantages women, there's a downside to the career mandate for men too. Succeeding is a slippery scale—there's always more that could be done; always some other man who's providing more for his family. Also, the career mandate contributes to men missing out on a lot of the intimate time with their own children. It's common for men on their deathbeds to regret not having spent more time with their families. Women rarely have this regret.

We need a coming together of the polarities of the motherhood mandate and career mandate. Both women and men need to give high priority to spending time with their families when considering careers and work in order for America to be strong in its families. And both men and women need to have equal opportunities in the workforce for there to be gender equality in the culture overall and in our homes. Couples who have gender equality report the highest levels of marital satisfaction and the lowest levels of depression.[34] For there to be equal opportunities in the workforce, husbands and wives must be making fair decisions in the home—not just decisions that favor the man's work.

What Families Need From Employers

Unfortunately, many Americans, like most in this study, have to make compromises between their work and their families. They have to sacrifice greater pay in order to spend more time with their families, or in order to live in an area they consider optimal for their families. Others sacrifice time with their families in order to pursue a career. What is also unfortunate is that many Americans see this forced choice as inevitable and they make their choices, and sacrifices, based on options they see around them. Consequently, with the "traditional" gender break down, dad usually gives up time with his family to pursue his career and bring home that all-important paycheck, and mom gives up her career for a job (that requires less of her time but also pays her less) in order to prioritize her children's and husband's needs.[35]

But at the same time, enough parents (particularly mothers) have voiced their concerns about demanding workplaces to the point that many companies have responded. In order to attract high quality workers, American businesses have implemented "family friendly" programs in recent years. Flextime and flexplace, have become increasingly available where businesses let workers set their own hours or work offsite as long as they get their work done. Job sharing is another innovation, where two workers share one full time position including responsibilities, pay and benefits. Generally this is good news, but recognize that these policies along with others like on-site daycare and family leave aren't in place because our culture values the family, it's because it values productivity. Companies have learned that family friendly policies reduce employee turnover and absenteeism. Yet, even if it's not for the purest of motives, increasingly companies are adding family friendly policies.

People with good educations and a vision for what could be available to them can move to some of these family friendly jobs. Many parents (both women and men) in my study chose teaching jobs in order to be accommodating of their children's school schedules. But at least one third of the men didn't seem to have a vision for a family-friendly job. For instance, because Ike lacked a college education but still desired to be the sole breadwinner of the family, he chose the marines and was shipped overseas, away from his family and into harm's way. Willie chose to work long hours for a corporation that transferred him and his family far from home. Sid chose a field that didn't pay well but was extremely emotionally taxing and Mike excuses his long work hours as just the nature of his field. In all four of these cases, the men don't seem to be able to (or are unwilling to) "think outside the box" in order to look for a job that would accommodate their families more.

While there is movement in our country toward having work become more "family-friendly." The reality for many is that it's not. Not enough American jobs offer paid maternity leave and even fewer offer paid paternity leave. Western Europe and Australia are showing the US that paid family leave can be provided to every full time worker. European countries provide at least six weeks at 60 percent pay with Scandinavian countries providing up to two years at 90 percent pay (and for the fathers too!).

In fact, a 2007 McGill University study of 173 countries found that the United States, Liberia, Swaziland, Papua New Guinea and Lesotho were the only countries that did not guarantee any paid maternity leave. Obviously, if 168 countries can do it, we can too—if we decide we value a mother's time with her newborn. Fortunately, California has taken the lead in the US on this matter. In 2004, Family Leave became state law. Workers are provided six weeks at 55% pay for maternity and paternity leave and elder care as well as other family needs. It is paid for through payroll deductions averaging $26 a year per worker. Hopefully other states will follow suit.

None of the people in my study suggested that a way their jobs or their spouses jobs could be supportive would be to supply paid family leave. We just don't realize it's feasible. Similarly, only two suggested on-site child care and options like flextime and job sharing didn't even come up. The first step toward more supportive jobs is the awareness that American workplaces could make changes that would aid families without compromising productivity.

Lastly, we do have choices about how a parent who "chooses" to be the one who compromises his—or more often, her—career is treated in the home. What commonly happens is the parent with the greater income gets certain privileges in the home: The best chair in the family room, possession of the remote, time to relax while the other parent takes care of dinner, children or cleaning. Kids pick up on this inequality in the home and make assessments about what it means. Some either consciously or unconsciously think that men are the ones who should be able to have both a career and a family while women are viewed as selfish if they pursue a career. Or perhaps they think that the career comes at a greater personal cost for the woman. They'll be less likely to question why women pay the costs but men don't if this was the norm in their own household.

Who's Minding the Kids?

All families face the crucial challenge of childcare while the parents are working for pay. Fewer and fewer families work this out by having the mother drop out of the workforce to care for the children full time. However, with the increasing number of women joining and staying in the workforce, a couple of logical questions arise: Who's taking care of the kids? And, are they being well taken care of?

In answer to the first question, census data reveal that 64 percent of mothers with children under six years old work for pay, about half of whom are working full time, year round[36]. So, we can assume that 36 percent of mothers are taking care of their children all of the time. Another four percent of children are cared for by their stay-at-home fathers. Of course, these mothers and fathers need breaks and they typically get them from their spouses, mothers, friends and church nurseries as well as childcare while they do activities such as aerobics. Very few people question the value of having these other people intermittently care for a mother's children. In fact, most see the value of having a number of caring adults share childcare responsibilities.

Twenty-seven percent of children with two working parents are being taken care of by a parent all of the time. Either the parents are taking turns with shifts so one is left to mind the kids, or the mother is taking care of her child while she works. For instance, she may bring other children into her home to babysit or she may work as a daycare worker where her child stays. Another 27 percent of the children are being taken care of by a relative in the child's or the relative's home.

CARE PROVIDERS FOR CHILDREN UNDER SIX YEARS OLD[37]

	Of all children under 6
Taken care of by mother full time	36%
Taken care of by father full time	4%
27% Of the 60% with two working parents are cared for by parents all the time	16.2%
27% Of the 60% with two working parents are cared for by parents and other relatives	16.2%
Children who are being cared for by one of their parents or another relative all of the time	———— = 72.4%

These methods of balancing work and family have been used for centuries by most cultures. Before the Industrial Revolution, both men and women were involved in the productive labor for the household, either through farm work or by making products such as chairs, candles, and clothes. The children of these men and women would be looked after by relatives or neighbors, and at early ages, they would be put to work. Tribal cultures also involve their children in productive labor at an early age and share the child care among available adults. It's from this type of culture that we've learned the very true African proverb, "It takes a village to raise a child." Only in recent times (the past 150 years) have we developed the notion that children should be at home with their mothers, full time. About 4% of children of working mothers are being taken care of by a nanny or babysitter in the child's home. (Women who come to the United States from other countries in order to be nannies are often surprised at the intensity of attention their employers expect them to give to the children.[38]) And 14 percent of children of working mothers are cared for in a care provider's home.

Only 16.8% of all children are in organized day care centers. That's a number considerably lower than I would have guessed before doing the research! These centers are where much concern is centered. Reports of abuse and neglect pepper the nightly news, raising the fear of such centers. However, the media create an exaggerated fear of organized daycare, and one must remember that the media more often report parental abuse and neglect. Research has revealed that there are good day care centers and bad day care centers. Middle class day care centers tend to be better than those in lower class neighborhoods.

Choosing a Quality Childcare Provider

For Fallon and Frank, choosing a quality daycare center was easy. After having their first child, they moved back to Fallon's home town and put their babies in the same daycare center where Fallon worked as a teenager. "It's like they're with family," says Frank. Similarly, Mary and Mike used their employer's onsite daycare center without a moment's concern since they knew many others who had used this reputable facility. Other parents may need to scrutinize daycare centers in order to find one that offers high quality care. By interviewing parents who have their children there and dropping in unannounced both before and after your own child is there, a lot can be ascertained.

Traits to look for in a childcare center include:

♦ **Ratio of children per worker. Child development experts generally recommend that there be at least one caregiver responsible for no more than 3 or 4 infants and toddlers (birth to 2 years old) or 6 or 7 preschool-aged children (between 2 and 5 years old).**

♦ **Is it clean?**

♦ **Does it have a good reputation? Ask teachers, neighbors, other parents, and others such as church friends in order to get a feel about a child care provider.**

♦ **How do the children spend their time? The American Pediatric Association recommends no television for children under two, so you may want to find a place that doesn't even have a television. Is there an outside play area?**

♦ **Is it safe?**

♦ **Are there structured games and activities? Some parents want to have a Montessori or other preschool curriculum for their children. This can be fine as long as the children don't feel pressured to learn. At this young age, there is little need to prepare them**

for school. We don't want to "turn them off" or frustrate them. However, if they're enjoying learning, find a place that gives them plenty of opportunity.
♦ **Are there scheduled and enforced rest times?**

An important way to have a good experience with a childcare center is to minimize the number of hours your child is spending there. Even as adults, we're tired at the end of the day and children wear-out much faster. When my twins were three, they started preschool for 2.5 hours a day, twice a week. (We also used a babysitter in our home for another 20 hours a week.) When they got home at 11:30, they would be so tired that they'd go straight in for a nap before eating lunch!

A large study on the effects of daycare on children was done several years ago. It found that five year olds who had been in daycare over 30 hours a week performed better in kindergarten than children who were not. It also found a slight tendency for the children in daycare long hours each week to be more aggressive. Consider your child's temperament in weighing the relative merits of a daycare situation for him or her.

A quality organized daycare center can provide advantages over in-home care. These include,

♦ **TV is used very sparingly**
♦ **They often have an organized preschool curriculum**
♦ **They can be relied on to have substitutes when a worker is sick (while a parent must take off work if a babysitter is sick.)**

Fifty-three percent of the families in my study had used organized daycare centers at one time or another. This number includes the families with stay-at-home moms, all of whom used Mothers' Day Out at local churches. Overwhelmingly, these families had positive experiences with the daycare centers. But, sadly, one family suspected that abuse had happened.

Another popular choice for childcare was for children to be taken care of in another person's home. Karen has used the same in-home care for five years with both of her children. She's very pleased with the care, adding that "they get hot lunches." Elyse has used two such arrangements successfully over the years. Vivian and Vincent have also used the same in-home care and also mentioned the hot lunches. Their son is now in kindergarten and their daughter spends long hours at the babysitter since both Vivian and Vincent have commutes of at least an hour each way. They are satisfied with the care, though they mention that "the TV is probably on too much." The TV being on too much is also a problem in many American households, with reports averaging 5-7 hours/day.

However, one family had an experience with in-home care that caused her some concern. Sometimes Pam would walk in to pick up her infant—at a home where two women cared for twelve children—and find her in her carrier. "Who knows, they may have held her for three hours and then just put her in (the carrier), but it seemed like she was there or the play pen or the car seat or the walker every day." So, after 9 months, she arranged to have her sister care for Christie at her house. "The love that my sister was able to give her sincerely, you can't even compare it." Pam reminds us how, after initially finding a center, parents must continually monitor the care. Remember too that quality child care providers can help parents. Many actually have much more experience with children than parents do and those in licensed facilities are required to get training every year. Consequently they can advise parents on how to deal with issues as varied as separation anxiety to biting.

This chapter has addressed the difficulties and time struggles that work causes us in our families. However it's important to remember that, all in all, American parents are doing a good job with their children. Fathers are spending more time interacting with their children than their own fathers and grandfathers did. Mothers continue to give high rates of interaction time with their children despite the time that they work more for pay than their mothers and grandmothers. (They sacrifice their sleep, clean house and leisure to do so!) Chapter 7 discusses another powerful influence on our families: The Media.

QUESTIONS TO ASK YOURSELF AND DISCUSS

When parents choose to work more than forty-five hours a week, they need to give serious thought as to why.

♦ **Is it because your family truly needs the money? For many, this is the case. But for others, they are prioritizing a new boat or a larger home or a bunch of trips to restaurants over time with their children. Be honest about your motivation and realize that kids need to be around both parents.**

♦ **Is it because you are in danger of losing your job if you don't put in the extra time? Again, this is a reality for some people. Others, however, choose to think their job is on the line when in fact they just need to set stronger boundaries at work. Your spouse may be able to help you to sort through what's true in your case.**

♦ Are you working more hours because of your personal drive for advancement? If so, recognize that children aren't young forever. Put off your own drive in favor of your children for now. There will be plenty of time later for you to pour yourself into your work. Writing this reminds me of Cat Stevens' old song, "The Cat's in the Cradle." Do you know it? It's about a man who always puts off spending time with his son while the boy is growing up—there's always something important the dad needs to do. His son grows up and has a family of his own and now it's the dad asking for the time and the son who always has other things he needs to do. The song ends with saying with a note of irony and disappointment, "My boy is just like me."

♦ Are you taking the easy way out? Arlie Hochschild's study of employees at a Fortune 500 corporation revealed that people often chose to go to work early and stay late simply because it was an easier place to be than home—more restful, even. At work, you could sit down and drink coffee for a moment's peace before your shift started. At home, there's always something else to be done—a lunch to make, a homework assignment to check, or a sibling fight to break up. Hochschild notes that men have been using work as an escape from home for a long time, but now women are starting to do it too, leaving the home underattended.

♦ It's understandable to need a break from the kids but if you're away more than forty-five hours, realize your kids need to be with you and your spouse probably needs a break!

Chapter 7

Seeing is Believing

Television, Movies and Family

In a commercial for a flu medication, the mother is sick in bed and Dad is tending to the kids: Feeding them sugar for breakfast and approving clothes that don't go together in color or pattern. Then we see the kids leave in their summer clothes, out into a snowy blizzard. Back inside, Dad fidgets helplessly in the very messy kitchen and then again in the overflowing laundry room. His one effort is to turn a toppled bottle back right side up. Even well into the 21st century an old joke is still being used: When it comes to housework and childcare, Dad is helpless.

Stories such as this one told through television and movies—even though we know they are fiction— affect the way we think about people and situations. Furthermore, what we watch affects our values.[39] In most American homes, the television is on at least seven hours a day, with people watching for three hours on average. American living rooms are focused on the television, homes have cable, satellites, DVRs, and DVDs. We can watch TV on our cell phones, on airplanes, on iPods and in numerous waiting rooms. We cannot escape television or the myths about family that it imparts. Scenarios like the joke on Dad in the flu medication advertisement persist despite the fact that we've had increasing numbers of stay-at-home dads for fifteen years, not to mention the norm that has developed of fathers being more involved than the fathers of the 1960s and 70s. For instance, when I picked up my kids from elementary school (a task that, because of our work schedules, I did one day a week while my husband did it four) it wasn't uncommon to see fathers picking up their children. No longer are fathers relegated to the Little League and Boy Scout sidelines in order to have interaction with their kids.

Still, the perceptions of fathers as being not-as-good parents often affect the household. Adam, who handles emergencies for a living, excused himself from the idea of taking turns with his wife taking days off from work when the baby was sick by saying he didn't know what to do with a sick baby. Where his self-concept as a worker would have him rise to the task at work, his self-concept as a father tells him it's okay to "pass" when he feels incompetent at home. Mothers, on the other hand, are more likely to feel the cultural pressure—continually conveyed in the media and everywhere else—to perform these tasks, to learn to be good at them. Many mothers do not feel like these skills come naturally at all. They learn because they're required to. As cultural perceptions change to expect men to be equally involved parents, their abilities with sick babies, nurturance and housework will improve.

Yet television consistently portrays stereotypic roles for females and males. Programs carefully script what men should do and what women should do, even if other role expectations would serve us better. These dramas are played out and reinforced in our daily conversations. For example, women who see the flu medication commercial complain by the water cooler or at the play group about how they are overworked. Such complaints reassert their value as wives and mothers.

All of this can seem relatively innocuous, and indeed compared to many of life's threats, they are. But the messages we unreflectively watch and listen to in the media can keep our families from operating at their best. Consider Russell Baker's comment in *The Awful Truth:*

> Among the privileges enjoyed by rich, fat, superpower America is the power to invent public reality. Politicians and the mass media do much of the inventing for us by telling us stories which purport to unfold a relatively simple reality. As out tribal storytellers, they shape our knowledge and ignorance of the world, not only producing ideas and emotions which influence the way we lead our lives, but also leaving us dangerously unaware of the difference between stories and reality.[40]

I continually find this statement to be true when listening to my students describe the way "families have always been." Their notions about breadwinner fathers and stay at home moms dating back to the cavemen have no empirical evidential support. Rather, my students' knowledge about "traditional" families comes largely from the media, from Fred Flintstone to Rush Limbaugh.

Television's Portrayals of Families

While most of us realize that television shows are not actual reflections of reality, we must also remember that what is depicted on television tells us something about what we value, otherwise, we wouldn't be watching. In general, we are much more interested in watching people's work lives than their family lives on TV, and we don't seem to be interested in watching how people mesh work and family together either. Katharine Heintz-Knowles reviewed 150 episodes of 98 television shows in order to analyze how prime time television depicts work and family issues.[41] She found that only about one third of prime time mothers work outside of the home compared to three-quarters in real life.   Moreover, television parents who have young children are seldom shown doing childcare and half the time viewers don't know what the childcare arrangements are during times when the parents are working.   Additionally, TV shows rarely show conflict between work and family but when they do, the conflicts are easily resolved.   These conflicts are portrayed as being the fault of the family, not the workplace. Yet the reality is that work and family conflicts are everyday occurrences for people with young children. But, interestingly, the expectant parents I interviewed didn't expect work-family conflicts at all.   Certainly, the purpose of television shows is to entertain but even if it's not intentional, television is also influencing people's perception of reality.

Television shows are considerably less stereotypical than they were in previous decades.   But shows from the past are still airing on television and influencing young families today. *Leave it to Beaver,* which originally aired from 1957-1963 and is still common among re-runs, is extremely stereotypical by today's standards. Ward Cleaver, sole breadwinner and disciplinarian for the family, was an accountant. His wife June was a stay-at-home mom who served well-balanced meals and vacuumed the living room in heels and pearls. They had two boys, adolescent Wally and young Theodore (Beaver) who engaged in mild misbehavior. The series followed the family through the events of everyday life, yet the storylines were quite avant guarde for their time, covering topics such as divorce and alcoholism.[42]

By the 1980s, television had considerably expanded its depictions of American families. Depicting two-parent, working class families, *The Simpsons* and *Roseanne* (in reruns) are still popular on television. Much loved for its humor through hyperbole, *The Simpsons* depicts the traditional male breadwinner and stay at home mom. Like June, Marge is submissive to her husband, but Homer, unqualified for his job and generally clueless, is nothing like Ward. *Roseanne* touches on the difficulties working class people face in providing financially for families. Both Dan and Roseanne Conner worked a number of different jobs over the years and Roseanne was the dominant personality in the marriage and the family.

Another popular show in syndication, *Home Improvement* which was originally produced for eight years in the 1990s, featured Tim "the Tool Man" and Jill Taylor and their three sons (males are depicted in lead roles twice as often as females in television and movies). Reflecting traditional gender roles with some modern twists, the show depicts Tim as host of his own home improvement show on cable television and Jill went back to school during the series to obtain her Master's degree in psychology. Audiences are exposed to a wider array of family elements than in *Leave it to Beaver*, including pillow talk, discussion about finances, disciplining the children, and work. Tim demonstrates affection with his wife and children much more than Ward. Also, the relationship between Tim and Jill includes squabbling and compromising, often with the help of their neighbor, Wilson, who gives sage advice to Tim. Ironically, the advice Wilson offered to Tim mirrored what Jill had already said. The boys all had a positive relationship with their father and would even participate in group hugs together. From this show, we learned that men are allowed to have deep and positive relationships with other men, and with their children. We also see more shared decision making, particularly between the spouses.

Stereotypes in Family Situation Comedies in TV and Movies

One avenue taken by comedy is to exploit common stereotypes. We all know these characters are not realistic but those images we watch and listen to have a powerful effect on our memories and perceptions to the point that research reports that people who watch a lot of television have more stereotypic views than people who don't. On one hand, we may see ourselves in these characters and laugh but on another, there may be a willingness to excuse dysfunctional behavior as "that's just the way men are" or "just the way women are." Some of the themes young parents have been continually exposed to are described here. Paying attention to how these are stereotypes and don't have to define our behavior helps us to move beyond the constrictions these roles place on us, which helps us to have more enjoyable families.

◆ Fathers are Inept

A common theme in family-centered situation comedies is that of an inept father. More foolish and less capable than his own children, Homer Simpson reigns as the archtype of inept father, but George Lopez and Ray Barone in *Everyone Loves Raymond* also portray incompetent fathers and husbands. For example, Ray's wife, Debra, often uses the word "idiot" to describe him. He has no idea how to handle the children and says insensitive things to Debra. In one particular episode, Debra asks Ray to take care of the twins (7 year-old boys) for the day. He already has plans to play golf and instead of changing his plans as she insists, he simply takes the boys with him. At the end of the day, the boys come home covered in dirt and grass stains from retrieving Ray's golf balls. Debra is incensed that Ray would take the children to the golf course with him. Ray's parents are present for this exchange and Ray tells about Frank taking Robert and him to the lodge instead of the playground when they were boys. There the boys would drink the foam off the top of Frank's beer, which he insists made a "man out of 'em. Almost." In the end, Debra gives in and admits that the boys seemed to have had a great time. However, it is still clear that Ray did not behave as Debra thinks a father should, illustrating another popular sentiment about fathers: They're the fun ones and mothers get stuck with the work.

◆ Mothers are Better Parents

Another idea that viewers sometimes unknowingly digest from television is the idea that mothers are more competent and caring parents than fathers. In another episode of *Everybody Loves Raymond* Debra and two of the three children are sick. Ray must take his daughter and the twin that is sick to the doctor. When he takes the children in for their examination, the doctor begins to ask Ray questions about the children. He asks about their sleeping habits, what they have been eating recently, and if they have been around other children who are sick. Ray does not know the answer to any of the questions. When it is time to examine the twin, the doctor looks at him and says "this child isn't sick. He's just fine." Seconds later, Ray's brother, Robert, walks in with the sick twin and trades Ray for the healthy twin. Ray's incompetence is completely apparent in this episode. He does not know about his children's recent behavior, as evidenced in his inability to answer questions, and he cannot even tell his own twin sons apart. We laugh at the situation because it is meant to be funny. The stereotype of incompetent fathers is exaggerated in this situation for the purpose of comedy. If Debra had taken the children to the doctor with the same results, it wouldn't be funny. As the mother, she is expected to know all of the answers to questions about her children. The unfortunate byproduct of this comedic situation is that it excuses men for being so unaware—it is seen not as a bad thing, it is a *funny* thing and a man thing.

We also see a more caring mother in *The Simpsons*. Even though it is a cartoon, it is targeted to an adult audience and has been on the air since 1989. The mother, Marge Simpson, is loving, caring, and even dotes on her children. The father, Homer, often forgets his youngest child's name (Maggie) and sometimes forgets that she exists, exclaiming "We have *three* children?".

Another example of a mother more competent than dad is in the *Cheaper by the Dozen* movies. Tom, the father of twelve children, is a football coach and his wife, Kate, is a stay-at-home mom. In the first *Cheaper by the Dozen*, Kate sacrifices her career in order to be a stay home with her kids full time. Then, supporting the cultural notion of supermom, somehow Kate manages to write a book while caring for 12 kids and running a household. Tom, on the other hand, is a mess. He loves his children, but it is clear that the mother is a better parent. Tom gets caught up in a competition with a peer, involves his children in pranks, and follows one of his daughters on her date, only to get into a fight with her date's father (who has also followed the couple). The two men are thrown out of the theater. Kate has to constantly work damage control to make up for Tom's mistakes. We do see positive traits in Tom though. For instance, Tom took a significant pay cut for returning to a less demanding job in order to spend more time with his family. Yet when it comes to nurturing, he will never be as good as Kate.

◆ The Man's Work is More Important

In situations where both parents work, the man's work is seen as more important than the woman's. Again, *Cheaper by the Dozen* serves as an example. In the first movie, Tom works while Kate stays at home. When Kate does get an opportunity to nurture her career, Tom is supportive of her going on a book tour. But chaos ensues as a result of Tom's attempt to juggle his job of coaching football and being a parent to twelve children.

Kate returns home during the middle of her tour, cutting it short, to return her family to order.

Some movies, like *The Rookie* and *The Astronaut Farmer* take the centrality of the husband's job to the extreme where the whole family makes huge sacrifices to support the father's unrealistic and selfish dream. *Freedom Writers,* on the other hand illustrates that this precedence of the man's vision does not apply to women's causes. Based on a true story, *Freedom Writers* tells of Erin Gruwell's accomplishments in an underachieving high school English class. Her work becomes consuming and she works two extra jobs to fund field trips for her students. Her husband Scott is in a stagnant job and feels overshadowed by Erin and her dedication to her students. He tells Erin "I can't be your wife," suggesting that husbands shouldn't be expected to support their wife's career the way wives support husbands. Scott feels that his role as husband should allow him to have a more prestigious position and Erin has taken this away from him with her hard work and success.

♦ It's Better if Mom Stays at Home

The fact that mothers are depicted as stay-at-home moms twice as often as real life illustrates television's ideal on this matter. Of course, this was most evident in TV shows of the 1950s like *Leave it to Beaver, Ozzie and Harriet* and *I Love Lucy.* In *I Love Lucy,* even before being a mother, Lucy was expected to stay at home and the show continually communicated the negative effects of a woman wanting to work. In addition to nagging Ricky for him to let her be a part of his show, Lucy's jobs always ended in disaster. Ricky did not want Lucy to work and always had to bail her out of her failed attempts at employment. Her most famous working blunder was her stint at the candy factory working at the conveyor belt. She could not keep up with the pace of the belt and began to stuff the candy in her shirt, her hat and her mouth. It was clear from this and other episodes that Lucy was not (and perhaps no woman was) cut out for the working world. In the candy factory episode, Lucy and her best friend Ethel got jobs and their husbands Ricky and Fred took over the housework. Not only did the women fail, but the men made a mess out of the cooking, further supporting the idea that a woman's place was in the home and a man's in the workplace.

Some shows over the years have been successful at countering these traditional stereotypes. Most noted for its positive contribution of depicting an upper-middle class African American family, *The Cosby Show* confronts gender stereotypes as well. Both Claire (an attorney) and Cliff (a physician) Huxtable work as professionals and both share equally in the parenting of the children. Some might argue that the show glosses over the demands of these two professions but both of these professions can be family-friendly if the workers are willing to make less income than their colleagues.

The 21st century has continued the trend of showing more women in the workplace and fathers in more nurturing roles as parents. While not in the majority, some television shows address work and family issues more realistically. *The New Adventures of Old Christine* addresses current conflict between working moms and stay-at-home moms. Christine receives the stay-at-home moms' smug disapproval when she visits her son's school and the stay-at-home moms are the ones in power with the Parent Teacher Organization.

Other shows, too, like *Malcolm in the Middle* and *Medium* feature families where both parents have jobs, and where the fathers are actively involved with the nurturing of children. So while television has many stereotypic roles airing, some shows are better than others. Like choosing what to feed your family or who to care for your child, careful attention to what and who you select makes all of the difference. And like food and use of caregivers, quantity also matters.

Though edgier, *Modern Family* and *Desperate Housewives* retain some traditional gender stereotypes. The mothers on *Modern Family* don't work for pay but the show does present some of the "downsides" that come with being a stay-at-home mom. Claire, for example, is visited by an old work colleague and is jealous of her friend's successes. In classic situation comedy fashion, however, the story finishes with Claire being happy with her choice to leave her career, feeling that her friend's life wasn't as meaningful as her own. Claire's husband, of course, enjoys both a career and a family life. Interestingly, the show's gay couple, Cal and Mitchell are used more to address the difficulties of leaving the workforce. Consequently, *Modern Family* communicates that these are problems men have even though, in reality, many women struggle with them too. Issues the show presents such as how the non-paid parent isn't taken as seriously, the desire to be using their talents outside of the home and how going without a job for too long drives them crazy are all common experiences for stay-at-home moms too.

Desperate Housewives, on the other hand, does show some working mothers. Particularly Lynette and Tom characterize the difficulties of managing both work and family. While Lynette has been more successful with her career, she is often depicted as manipulative in getting her needs met. Tom, while supportive of his wife, is not an equal parent and the family sacrifices all of their financial resources for Tom to chase his pipedream of owning a pizza restaurant. Another character, Brea, has a successful career but she was a stay-at-home mom while her children were young, as are Gaby and Susan. None of the fathers on *Desperate Housewives* are very involved with their kids.

The content of television is certainly important to consider when discussing what affects our families but the practice of watching television needs to be addressed as well.

Watching TV

I recently conducted a little seminar on family relationships at a local church. As an ice-breaker, I had participants draw their dinner table and assign a color to represent their relationship with each person at the table. As people shared their drawings, a common denominator appeared: People had drawn in television sets! One person didn't even draw the dinner table but drew her family clustered around the TV in the "family" room. Dinner has a long and rich tradition of being a time people interact with one another. It's so important that religions around the world have meals together as part of their rituals—a time when people take the time to relax, "break bread" and talk to one another.

Watching television can be entertaining and can be a family activity. But watching too much television means that there are other things we're not doing. The U.S. Census Bureau reports that 98.2% of American households have at least one TV with the average per household being 2.4. Further, they estimate that adults are watching 4.6 hours of television each day—that's the equivalent of seventy days worth of television a year! Children watch even more.

Time watching TV is time we're not interacting much with others. Therefore, it's alarming to see that television has intruded on a traditional family time like dinner, when we take a moment to look at each other and share about our days. Not only can television interrupt our family communication, it can also keep us from exercising, playing and spending time outside—all activities that help us to be healthy and well-adjusted. Certainly watching TV together as a family can be a worthwhile family activity, providing entertainment, a common interest and opportunity to discuss topics the shows present. Common sense, pre-screening shows and asking others can help parents choose appropriate shows for viewing.

However, the American Pediatric Association recommends that children under two watch no TV at all. Their concern is primarily about brain development and a link that has been found with young children watching television developing ADHD when they get older. My students are often shocked to hear this and ask, "What about *Baby Einstein*?" Basically, we've overestimated the value of television as a learning tool. It can have a place for children over two, but nothing beats interaction with adults to stimulate their brain. Interaction includes everything from reading to them, playing, pretending, and building things using those brightly colored blocks with raised letters on them.

Turning off the TV also helps with a common disciplinary problem with children—bedtime. Parents often complain about how difficult it is to get their young one to go to bed, stay there and go to sleep. Sometimes the problem is caused by something as simple as TV. Since Sally has spent the last three hours semi-comatose in front of the tube, she's just not that tired when bedtime comes around. Turning the TV off and playing with her does both parent and child a world of good and helps them both go to sleep easier.

Watching Movies

Going to the movies is an enjoyable pastime. Like television, the content of the movies and the number of movies being consumed make the difference between movie watching being a good or bad experience. Like TV, movies are rated and this gives a thumbnail sketch regarding the suitability of the movie for our children and even ourselves. I've found Kids-in-Mind. com to be an excellent reference to use because it provides numbers to rate violence, sex/nudity and profanity. Additionally, it provides a narrative describing why the movie received the ratings it did in each category which allows the parents to decide whether they agree with the reviewer (not to mention the MPAA ratings). Personally, I think some movies that receive a PG-13 rating should be rated R and some rated R should be PG-13. Also, there are many movie guide books available that give suggestions for age suitability and even themes to discuss with your children after the movie is over. Or, if your kids are like mine, some of those discussions happen during the movie. Obviously, this needs to happen with movies you watch at home. When *Remember the Titans* first came out on video, our family had one of those teachable moments in the middle of the movie where the Black coach said to the White kid, "Who's your daddy?" and the White kid said, "You are."

My six year old exclaimed, "That's his daddy?!!" so we paused to explain how "who's your daddy" was an expression used to communicate trust and respect. The next section discusses two movies many young parents have seen more than once—The 1998 remake of *The Parent Trap* and *Snow Day* (2000)—to illustrate common myths about men's and women's "proper roles" with respect to work and family

Stereotypic Roles in Movies

In many ways *The Parent Trap* and *Snow Day* reflect the values and family structures of the late 20th century. For example, both movies depict working mothers which reflects the situations in a large majority (75%) of American households with school-age children. And, like many movies targeted to children and families, the children in these movies know best while parents and other adults often seem quite dense. Though the stories seem modern, both movies convey traditional gender roles. Fathers are expected to be successful in their careers but when mothers are successful at their work, the family suffers. For instance, in *Snow Day* the father in the family (Tom) is a meteorologist. Having accurately predicted snow, he leaves for work, hoping to get the credit he deserves. Meanwhile, Tom's teenaged son, Hal, wants to spend the snow day off from school vying for a girl's attention but his mom (Laura) tells him he must watch his younger brother (Randy) because she has an international, high dollar real estate deal to close that day. But when Laura can't get out of the garage because of the snow, Hal scurries out of the house saying, "Don't worry mom, at least you can get some quality time (with Randy)."

Laura is shown repeatedly trying to manage a videophone call via her computer. As she tries, we learn how Randy is closer to his babysitter than his mom or anyone else. Laura apparently is successful at work and this is shown to be in direct conflict with her being an effective mother. All she needs is an hour or two for this deal to go through but both father and son are too busy with their own issues to give her a hand with hers. She finally gives up when Randy throws her phone in the snow and starts playing with him. Consequently, the movie makes it seem like Mom's family success requires her work failure. Hal later refers to this incident as his mom's "getting her life back." But Tom's success at work is not shown to cause the family any difficulties.

Similar to *Snow Day*, *The Parent Trap* depicts a mother's success with her career causing her to be insensitive to her children's needs. Identical twins were separated at age one with each parent getting custody of one. At summer camp, the girls switch places and return home to their respective estranged parent. Though subtle, the mother's career success appears to be the reason she didn't recognize she was now with the child she had not seen in ten years. While work is often depicted as being in conflict with family for women, it isn't a conflict for men. In fact, it wasn't the father's career that got in the way of his recognizing his estranged child; it was his romantic relationship with a too-young woman that caused him to be blind as a parent. Both movies leave viewers with the implicit message that women cannot be effective mothers and successful career women while such a conflict doesn't exist for the men in these stories. This perspective is confusing, if not subversive, in a society where 75% of mothers with school age children work.

Other movies challenge traditional notions. *Daddy Day Care* began with the old stereotype that says men can't handle children but the men were transformed into competent caregivers. Movies like *Daddy Day Care* serve to create more positive images for fathers much the same way as they've increasingly portrayed women as competent workers in recent years. By being aware of cultural stereotypes illustrated in television and the movies and by discussing how men and women are portrayed, people can avoid being manipulated by mindless conformity to "the way it's always been" and create more dynamic and enjoyable experiences for everyone in the family. Chapter 7, Every Home is a Home School, continues our discussion of how good parents can become even better.

QUESTIONS TO ASK YOURSELF AND DISCUSS

What TV shows do you regularly watch?
What movies have you seen lately?
How do these shows and movies depict the roles of mothers and fathers?
How do they present issues related to work and family?

The Sun Also Rises

Chapter 8

Every Home Is a Home School

Parents are our first teachers. In fact, sociologists confirm that parents remain our primary teachers for the entire time we live with them, despite the influence of the media and schools. If we're lucky our parents will remain our important advisors until we're well into middle age.

Our country (and every other country, for that matter) depends on parents to raise their young to be responsible, hardworking adults—people who pay taxes and volunteer in the community. The Bible asserts the importance of parents' roles in Proverbs 22:6 saying, "Direct your children onto the right path, and when they are older, they will not leave it." Parents teach us morals, ethics, nutrition, how to have good relationships, and study skills. The list is endless and, contrary to popular opinion, they even teach technology! Consider some of the technology we teach our children, even once they're ten or twelve years old: If clothes are left in the washer and it's inadvertently turned back on, you can't throw the dripping wet clothes in the dryer—you have to run it through the spin cycle. And someone has to teach kids how to open frozen orange juice cans!

Our kids learn to cook and clean from us, we help them with their homework and most importantly, they learn how to be good people and how to live in a family from us. Our role modeling will affect them their whole lives just as our own parents' role modeling affects us. For instance, Bridget, a high school technology teacher, learned that her father got special consideration for being tired when she was growing up. He spent twenty-five years working as a pipe-fitter. Her mother worked full time as a secretary. Now with her own children, Bridget describes a way her new family with Brandon is similar to how she was brought up:

> [Brandon is] *tired when he comes home and has a tendency to push the kids away and just (say), "Leave me alone for a while." That's something that my dad did too. He came home and he was hot and tired. He didn't want to mess with us. He'd say, "Just go away for a while and when I'm ready for you . . ." And that's not his fault. It's just something that happens because of the time element and being out in the heat, things like that.*

Since Bridget learned in her home growing up that Dad is tired and needs his space, she is sympathetic to Brandon's situation. However, she doesn't give herself the same allowance to get space even though she also works full time with a long commute. Parents need to be sensitive to how they communicate different expectations for males and females in the household especially if they give privileges to one gender over another.

The parents in my study attested to the importance of their own parents' role modeling—usually in a positive way. Often, they cited their parents as instrumental in teaching them how to be good parents. Sometimes men talked about the problems with having dads as the disciplinarians. These men learned not to respect their mothers as much because the mothers didn't know how to make them toe the line. Kyle, a thirty year old journalist and father of two reflects on his own upbringing saying,

> *I told (my wife), I said, "I don't want to be the only disciplinarian." That was something from my background, 'cause my mother wasn't a disciplinarian. She'd say, "You wait 'til your father gets home." That's the bad guy, and I don't want to be the bad guy to my kids. "Your daddy's coming, you're gonna get it." I grew up living with that. I also didn't want, if we had boys (when we were talking about having kids) I also didn't want Karen to be run over by them. My mom could tell me something and I'd, 'ssffttt'. There were times that I did disrespect. . . I told Karen, "I want our children to respect you." You know, 'cause I didn't respect my mom. So it was important that she, that we both bear the weight of disciplinarian.*

Teaching Children to Behave

Kyle describes a common power play between parents and children when our attempts at discipline run awry. We want to avoid getting into these conflicts with our children as much as possible since they actually run against our purpose of teaching our children right behavior. Of course, the ultimate goal of discipline is to teach children how to successfully negotiate their world.

The best way to accomplish this task is to provide them an environment that helps them to be successful. When children are young, we need to anticipate ways the kids could get in trouble or misbehave and remove those opportunities from their options. As an analogy, imagine your child is traveling down the road of life. When they're young, we want to put our kids in a bumper car and pad both sides of the road. As they grow we can remove the padding as they become progressively better navigators and aren't in danger of driving off the road.

So, rather than focusing on how to punish a toddler who goes into the street, we never give him or her the opportunity. We can help our children successfully navigate the road of life by considering two seemingly contradictory truths:

1. Children have some of the same needs we have. Those needs just look different because of their age.
2. Kids don't look at the world the same way we do. They don't have as much life experience and they don't have the ability to think abstractly.

Of course, they'll still get in trouble, but the number of times will be greatly reduced if we consider three needs our children have: Expectations, control and attention. (These are needs we have too!)

We all have expectations and when our expectations aren't met, we feel disappointed or upset. As adults we sometimes lose sight of just how much we understand what's going on. We can reasonably predict a lot of our day. We know when we'll be eating, when we get to watch TV, when people are coming over—or why no one is coming over today. We also have an understanding of time. We've lived a long time and we've kind of gotten a handle on it.

But for toddlers, everything is new. They haven't really learned cause and effect and they certainly don't have much experience to draw from. When my kids were in preschool, the whole preschool came to our house for an Easter egg hunt. When it was over, one of the teachers said to Forrest, "Thanks for inviting us." Forrest responded, "We didn't invite you; you just came." She got a chuckle out of that. Even though Forrest had been told that the preschool was coming over, he had no past experience to compare this to and certainly didn't understand the event in terms of an invitation. Fortunately, children take many of these surprises in stride—especially when they're fun!

When we provide predictability for our kids, we reduce their anxiety and improve the likelihood of their good behavior. And when things *are* out of the ordinary, the more we can tell them what to expect, putting it into as concrete of terms as we can think of, the less opportunity for the kiddos to develop the anxiety that comes from not knowing. When our own kids were young, Christopher and I would try to think of everything we knew about a new situation that our toddlers didn't, and then tell them what to expect. At age three we introduced TV in the form of a *Barney* episode twice a day. We would use that to help them gage how long we would be in the car. "We're going to Fort Worth and it will take about as long as watching two *Barneys*." But of course, there were times when we screwed up. One time, a friend and I took our four preschoolers to a resort area. The kids sat confined in their car seats for 45 minutes, knowing that their reward would be swimming and going out to eat. I made my mistake with the order I listed the activities in: I said we'd swim and eat. My son, Parker, understandably thought we were going to swim first and was terribly disappointed when we pulled up at the restaurant. Now, he loves to eat at restaurants, but at age four, he saw them as another place where he had to sit still. Usually easy-going, he melted down because of incorrect expectations.

Now my kids are teenagers. They know a lot more but I find it still helps to verbalize what they can expect with everything from what happens when our airplane flight gets cancelled to what college will be like.

Control is something else we all need. Again, as adults we get a lot of it. But when there's a situation we care deeply about—where we feel like we have no say in how it works out—we feel sad, upset, even angry. In fact, one of the circumstances parents can get upset about is when they don't feel like they have control over their toddler! We actually get in power struggles with these little masters of psychological warfare and they definitely have the ability to cause us to lose our cool. So, as much as possible, we try to avoid getting to that stand-off. One way to reduce behavior problems is to provide children some age-appropriate control. Ask them if they would like peas or carrots for dinner. Or give them the choice between two outfits to wear. (Make sure they are choices you can live with.) With toddlers, it's also important to not overwhelm them with too many choices, but let them have say-so when you can. Again, how much we give our children changes as they age. We give them more control and sometimes have to give up our own, allowing them some opportunities to be their own person. Yet we maintain control when we need to, to protect them as we continue to teach them to navigate the road of life on their own.

Lastly, we all need attention. When we talk about children's misbehavior, we often emphasize how they will seek attention even if it's negative. Therefore, an effective way to avoid behavior problems is to give your child a thirty second burst of attention. Of course, they often need much more time than this, but even when you're in the midst of doing something important to you, thirty seconds often meets their need for attention and keeps them from misbehaving. For instance, when you're chatting with a friend and your child is pulling on your clothes, saying, "Mommy, mommy, mommy . . . , say, "Excuse me", and look your child full in the face and talk to him/her for thirty seconds. Use the end of that time to say it is now your friend's turn to have your attention.

Christopher and I would ask our toddlers, "Do you need some special attention?" and it was funny when they actually started feeding this back to us and hearing this little one saying, "I need some special attention." We would pick them up, give them a kiss and some eye contact, and soon they'd be good to go. As they got older, we would make them wait—when they were interrupting a conversation, for instance. I remember my six-year-old learning to wait his turn, being quiet, but jumping until I turned my sights to him. (He outgrew the jumping on his own ☺.)

This need for attention is capitalized upon with the "time out" method of discipline. With time outs, parental attention is actually removed. It doesn't work 100% of the time but research shows that it is as effective (or more) than any other disciplinary technique. When our kids were young, we were big proponents of time-outs. As they've become older, we remove TV or video game privileges rather than time with friends—or we add on extra chores rather than spanking or grounding.

Grounding a child from beneficial activities is antithetical to our overall goals as parents.

In the marriages I studied that seemed to be the most stressed, marital conflict over discipline was common. In all of these most stressed-out cases, mothers were frustrated that the fathers were not providing any discipline at all. These fathers spent long hours away from their children and didn't want to spend what little time they had with their kids enforcing good behavior. Indeed, you can see that these mothers were dealing with dashed expectations and feelings of a lack of control. Perhaps they also were not getting enough attention from their husband as well. Later in this chapter, I discuss how to move beyond these kinds of impasses in marriage. Having a good relationship with our spouse helps us as we seek to guide and teach our children. A good marriage, in fact, makes us better parents. The next section will describe elements present in a marriage that encourage the development of psychologically healthy children.

Five Characteristics of Marriages with Psychologically Healthy Children

Dr. Jerry Lewis, a psychiatrist at Dallas's Timberlawn Hospital, conducted a large study comparing the marriages of parents of psychologically troubled youth to the marriages of parents of youth who tested to be psychologically healthy. After interviewing 250 couples in each category, Dr. Lewis distilled his findings down to five factors that marriages possess which lead to developing psychologically healthy children.[43]

First, Lewis found that the healthiest marriages shared activities and friends (closeness). They did things together (their WE).

Second, they were committed to their marriages above everything else. That means both members of the couple prioritized their marriage before their work, their own parents, and even their children. Indeed, to be the best father you can be, you are the best husband you can be; to be the best mother you can be, you are the best wife you can be. Children try to divide the parents to conquer, but they're actually relieved when they can't (again, their WE).

Third, they share the tough stuff with each other (intimacy). People in the healthiest marriages say things like, "I can tell her anything." They can share with their spouses the stuff they've never told anyone; the stuff they're ashamed of. They know that this person will still love them and won't use this information against them in the future (a shared WE).

Fourth, they have the ability to go out and face the world alone (autonomy). The marriage gives each partner the strength to be separate from their spouse and to thrive (their ME).

Fifth, parents in marriages that produce the most psychologically healthy children have shared power. There is not one person who dominates the other (a sharing of the WE and the ME). The Apostle Paul provides instruction that can be aptly applied to parents, "Share each other's burdens, and in this way obey the law of Christ" (Galatians 6:2 NLT).

> **Take a moment, now, to reflect on your marriage. What would you say is its greatest strength?**

Lewis states that marriages embodying all five of these elements are highly functional and 95 percent of their children test as psychologically healthy. (We're talking about people here, so we'll never see 100 percent resulting from a mere five factors.)

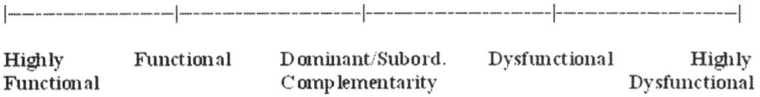

|------------------|------------------|------------------|------------------|

| Highly | Functional | Dominant/Subord. | Dysfunctional | Highly |
| Functional | | Complementarity | | Dysfunctional |

The next best marriages are those that have not involved their children in their problems. What they are missing is the closeness and intimacy. The parents are missing out on the good stuff, but the kids may not even realize it. Ninety percent of these kids test to be psychologically healthy.

About midway on Lewis's scale is "Dominant/Subordinate Complementarity." By this, he means that the spouses have agreed—either spoken or not—to have one spouse be the boss. Often, we think of this type relationship as the husband as the head of the house with the wife being submissive to him. Again, the couple may have decided this overtly or they may have just fallen into this pattern because of the way they were brought up. Lewis's idea also includes when the wife is the boss and the husband is okay with it. Lewis says children of parents with power imbalances often have trouble getting "launched" as young adults; they tend to doubt themselves. Even though the parents aren't in any kind of unpleasant conflict, the kids witness the imbalance of power. They tend to be more connected to the parent with the lesser power, which of course means they're not as close to the dominant parent. Sometimes, the parent with the least power colludes with the child against the powerful parent, as is illustrated with statements such as "Don't tell dad." It's easy to see how dad is being left out of the loop. When communication breaks down, so does intimacy.

In this typical scenario in which the father has been dominant, sons have less confidence when it's time for them to leave home; they're not so sure they can always make good decisions. This could be because their father didn't reveal the uncertainty he had when making tough decisions because revealing that would be admitting weakness. Daughters often look for some other man to make decisions for them—a boyfriend or preacher, for example.

On the dysfunctional side is the "conflicted" marriage where perhaps the couple's only strength is autonomy. The parents are in conflict with one another and the kids know it. The children may be expected to take sides. I'll use an illustration from America's oldest reality TV show. It was called "An American Family" and was aired on PBS in the 1970s. A California family with a sole breadwinner father, stay-at-home mother, and their five children agreed to have cameras set up in their home as well as to have an occasional cameraman follow them to activities. Two hours of their lives were aired every Sunday. It was the most successful series ever on PBS.

Over the course of the year, problems became evident. One problem was that the father was having an affair. After learning of the affair, the mother sent their teenage son to pick his dad up from the airport as he returned from a business trip. She told her son to tell his dad that she wanted a divorce. The next scene showed the three of them in the living room of their house. The mother seems to have begun the conversation about the divorce mid-paragraph and the father isn't following what she's talking about. The mother turns to the son and asks, "Didn't you tell him I was divorcing him?" The son says, "No." (Smart kid!) Obviously, this couple is conflicted and one of the problems in conflicted marriages is that the kids know their parents' problems and, as illustrated here, they are sometimes drawn into the middle of them. It's not surprising that such a situation causes negative effects on the child's well-being.

The most severely dysfunctional marriages take two forms. One form is a further extension of the conflicted marriages in which the parents are totally alienated. The spouses have their MEs with little to know WE. Some of these totally alienated couples are actually divorced (other divorced couples are actually more cooperative, which has positive effects on the children). The other form is what Lewis calls "fused symbiotic." Borrowing a term from biology, Lewis is describing a relationship that is so tight that each member of the couple actually feeds on the other, needing the other to survive. These individuals cannot function on their own. These two forms of severely dysfunctional marriages are on opposite ends of the pole regarding the spouse's dependency—either not nearly enough or way too much—but according to Lewis, either extreme results in only 10 percent of children testing to be psychologically healthy.

To summarize, as we seek to have marriages that produce psychologically healthy children, we begin by being psychologically healthy ourselves. This includes being someone who can face the world alone and has his/her our own hopes, needs and aspirations (our ME). We bond together with another autonomous person who has hopes, needs and aspirations, and we form a WE. In those marriages comprised of our balancing between our two MEs and our WE, we develop the characteristics that will make us the best parents we can be: Closeness, commitment, intimacy, autonomy, and shared power. These elements provide our foundation for good parenting. On that foundation, we want to add the building blocks of shared parenting.

Shared Parenting: The Benefits of Having Dad Involved Too

Wearing cowboy boots and driving a pickup truck, Greg is a regular at Home Depot. He's personally done a lot of the finishing of his family's new home. In these ways, Greg seems like the prototypical Texas man. But after revealing his ideas about marriage and parenting, Greg turns out to be a new kind of renegade—the type that bucks traditional gendered expectations. He describes how everyone wins when two parents are involved with child care:

> *I don't think that she should be stuck with the kids all the time. I think from our parent's generation the woman was the one who took care of the kids, raised the kids, and the guy went off and did what he wanted to do. Well, I think she ought to have time to go do what she wants to do, too, because she lets me do my thing, and we split it up. And I like taking the kids with me.*

Kids win when dad (as well as mom) is involved with them. They benefit from more parent time—something that research has shown directly relates to their well being. Having two involved parents is better than one. It doubles the parental resources for the children; they have two people to learn from. It also allows the parents to give each other breaks so that they can be emotionally present when they are with the kids. When children have two involved parents, they

- **Have higher self-esteem**
- **Are more resistant to peer pressure**
- **Have more empathy**
- **Do better in school**

Why is this? One reason is because children are exhausting both physically and emotionally. When parents can take turns with the childcare, they can renew their energy and are less likely to be impatient with the kids. So not only do children benefit, but mom also benefits by getting a break and having a partner who understands how taxing parenthood can be. Additionally, this involved partner is more informed when concerns about the children need to be discussed. These two are truly in it together. Last but not least, dad benefits from being involved. He gets to share the joy of being emotionally close to the kids. "I get razzed about doing so much with the kids," explains another involved father, "but I wouldn't have it any other way, 'cause that's how you get to know 'em."

Kid Pro Quo: Making Trade-Offs Solves Common Problems

Frequently women complain about their husbands not doing their fair share of the housework and childcare. Husbands defend themselves by saying they do more than their fathers did. Rosie and Robert illustrate a typical pattern.

Interviewer: *Do you expect the way you divide house work, paid work and childcare to change in the future?*

Rosie: *(pause) Noooooo. We've tried to make changes. I give my speech: "It's going to stay this way because this is all I'm going to get done. If you want more, you're going to have to do more." He does extra things for a while and then it goes back. So I think this is just our status quo and we just have to make the best of it.*

Robert, who sees himself as flexible, says nothing about the above when I interviewed him separately. When asked the same question, he replies, "Yes, because as the kids get older, they'll start doing things for themselves. We're already seeing that with Amber."

When I asked what had caused him and Rosie to split up paid work, childcare, and housework the way they had, Robert focused on explaining why he did so much more than his father and brothers rather than explaining why he didn't do as much as his wife. He explains that his job prevents him from doing more at home. Yet Rosie has an equally (or more) prestigious job that pays about the same. She thinks she is better at setting boundaries at her work than Robert is.

Rosie and Robert's situation is very common in families where both parents work, so common that John Stoessel addressed it in a *20/20* episode. He uses Robin and Cory as guinea pigs. Robin, an accountant who works thirty hours a week, and Cory, a radiologist with his own practice, have two elementary school aged children. Robin helps with the traditionally male role by bringing in extra income but Cory is far from picking up the slack at home. Stoessel points out that Cory functions more like an assistant parent than a parent, and not a very good one at that. Cory does pick up the kids from school a couple of days a week, while Robin works. But he does silly things that seem pretty ludicrous considering he's competent and smart enough to be a doctor. For instance, he lets his nine-year-old son do his math homework in pen and he forgets to pick up milk on the way home from work. When Robin takes the son to his cub scout meeting where she serves as den mother, Cory kicks off his shoes and watches TV, not putting away the pizza from supper, not vacuuming as Robin requested, and excusing his daughter from taking a bath. When considering both paid work and the unpaid work of housework and childcare, Robin, like many women, is clocking in about fifteen to twenty more hours a week than her husband. In sum, Cory underfunctions in the home, causing Robin to overfunction. Or, you could say Robin overfunctions in the home, allowing Cory to underfunction. It takes two to tango and these two have created their dance.

Stoessel and his guest parenting expert, Ron Taeffel, address some key issues, most notably that

- **the couple needs to be communicating more directly with one another;**
- **the husbands need to be taking more chores off their wives' "endless lists";**
- **the wives are going to need to give up some of the control and let their husbands do things their own ways.**

However, the show stops short of addressing the bigger picture in order for the change to be permanent. To their list, I would add,

- **both spouses are going to have to see the benefits in changing.**

There's an old joke: "How many psychiatrists does it take to change a lightbulb?" Answer: "One but it's going to have to really want to change." The same is true for Robin and Cory. They're really going to have to want to change. When I show this video clip to my marriage workshops and Sociology of the Family classes, I tell them that Robin and Cory created this situation for themselves. Consequently, there must be some benefits they see in it for themselves. So I ask my classes, what's in it for Cory for things to be this way? And what's in it for Robin? For Robin and Cory to change, they must be willing to give up the benefits of their current situation and desire the benefits of truly shared parenting. Here's what people often offer as the benefits Robin and Cory currently receive: Robin gets things done her way, she benefits from being emotionally closer to the kids and, (some astute student will note), she gets to be the martyr. She gets credit for being the one doing more than her share and that makes her feel good about herself. I admit this concept is easy to miss. One time I was talking to an acquaintance who was describing how she had to do all of the cleaning for her husband and three teenage sons because they spent all of their free time hunting and fishing. I suggested that the boys could be doing their own laundry (addressing one of her specific complaints) but my suggestion was completely dismissed as she continued her litany of grievances. Next, I suggested they get a maid to help her out, since these people are quite comfortable financially. Again, my idea was dismissed and it was only at this point that I got the message: My role was to say, "Poor you." She didn't want help. She wanted appreciation.

My workshop participants suggest that Cory benefits from more free time, less responsibility at home and that feeling of being "king of the castle"—entitled to sit down and relax even while his wife keeps working. Since Robin and Cory are going to have to see the benefits of changing for there to be a permanent change, the next step is to identify what those benefits might be. For instance, Robin could have more free time and less responsibility. She would have to decide that these benefits are more important than the control and the martyrdom. Cory would gain the appreciation of his wife, more closeness with the kids, and probably some self-respect. For both of them, they would increase the emotional intimacy in the marriage since they would be sharing the common task of parenting. If both partners become conscious of how their lives can improve by making some changes in the way they do housework and childcare, they are much more likely to make these changes last.

Saint Paul provides us some basic truths that can be applied to this situation using the metaphor of the Body of Christ in First Corinthians 12.

[14] Yes, the body has many different parts, not just one part. [15] If the foot says, "I am not a part of the body because I am not a hand," that does not make it any less a part of the body. [16] And if the ear says, "I am not part of the body because I am not an eye," would that make it any less a part of the body? [17] If the whole body were an eye, how would you hear? Or if your whole body were an ear, how would you smell anything? [18] But our

bodies have many parts, and God has put each part just where he wants it. [19] How strange a body would be if it had only one part!

One application of this passage is to say, "Men, you're important too!" There's no reason to say, "Since I'm not a mother, I don't matter with the nurturing of my children." Paul continues by saying,

> [21]The eye can never say to the hand, "I don't need you." The head can't say to the feet, "I don't need you." [22] In fact, some parts of the body that seem weakest and least important are actually the most necessary. [23] And the parts we regard as less honorable are those we clothe with the greatest care. So we carefully protect those parts that should not be seen, [24] while the more honorable parts do not require this special care. So God has put the body together such that extra honor and care are given to those parts that have less dignity. [25] This makes for harmony among the members, so that all the members care for each other.

He helps us to remember that we are not better than our spouse and don't deserve special privileges that the other doesn't have.

In the last part of this passage, Paul states, "[26] If one part suffers, all the parts suffer with it, and if one part is honored, all the parts are glad." Here he reminds us again, to bear one another's burdens. If you are the legs, help the back out in lifting that load!

QUESTIONS TO ASK YOURSELF AND DISCUSS

Robin and Cory are doing the overfunctioner/underfunctioner dance. Do you and your spouse have a common "routine" that leaves you dissatisfied? Identifying your dance is the first step in correcting your dance steps.

Here are some common parent dances:

- ♦ **The overfunctioner/underfunctioner tango (like Robin and Cory)**
- ♦ **The discipline mambo (where one parent enforces the rules while the other parent prefers to be a playmate)**
- ♦ **The I want WE time, you want ME time shuffle (Like Lance and Laurie in chapter 4)**
- ♦ **The not-so-traditional two step (Mom is at home but Dad hardly ever is, like Olivia and Oscar in chapter 5)**

Once you've identified your dance, answer these questions:

1. **What are the negative effects of the current arrangement (dance)?**
2. **What does each of you get out of the current arrangement (dance)?**
3. **How would each of you benefit by changing the way you're doing things (starting a new dance)?**
4. **What would it cost you?**
5. **Is it worth it to you to change? If not, what would make it worthwhile to you?**

Why Dads are Often More Fun

It's become popular to say "Mothers and fathers parent differently and that's okay." While I agree with this statement, people often seem to overlook *why* mothers and fathers parent differently. A major reason is that mothers have been assigned the ultimate responsibility for the child's welfare. You can hear it on the news when they report, "A baby has been found, abandoned by his mother." That baby was abandoned by his father too.

Having the ultimate responsibility for the child's welfare causes mothers to become task-oriented. Fathers often feel that their primary responsibility is for bread-winning and usually take the role of helper at home. Being the helper allows them to feel freer to play and have fun with the kids. Consider this story relayed to me by a grandmother. At dinner one night, her daughter became insistent that her two-year-old, Brittany, eat some meat. Brittany, having decided to go on an all-fruit diet, said, "Me eat no chicken." At this point, Brittany's dad noticed a mounting conflict at the dinner table and said, "Let's all take a bite of chicken," and all of the adults at the table took a bite of chicken and said, "Mmmm." Then dad said, "Let's all take another bite of chicken." This time Brittany joins in and before long she asks for chicken.

We all celebrate the wisdom of this method of parenting and commend dads like Keith above for coming up with such a fun way to get Brittany to eat meat. How wonderful it is that Keith gets involved rather than being like the dad on TVs *Still Standing*, sitting back and making mom do all of the parenting, conflicts and all. But what allows Keith to have this playful insight into conflict resolution actually happened because he is not ultimately responsible for Brittany's diet. If Brittany ends up malnourished, the TV news will lay the blame on her mother. That freedom leads to dad's ingenuity. As dads take on more of the responsibilities of their children's diet, sleep, baths, clothes, and so forth, moms will be freer to become more playful parents.

Making Your Home a Great Home School

Moms and dads share the common goal of bringing up their children to be psychologically healthy, content, and productive adults. Parents naturally are put into this situation together. By having a good marriage, we are emotionally strengthened and can work as a team to provide a supportive, nurturing atmosphere where we provide guidance and discipline for our children.

However, parenthood causes us to fall short on two important commodities: time and money. Having children causes parents to have less leisure time and even less sleep. We also have less expendable income than we used to. When there are not enough resources (time and money) to go around, a competition can develop, so the two parents who are supposed to be on the same team with a common goal may be operating more like competitors. Our kids are watching when we engage in these competitions, so we may be inadvertently sending them wrong messages about what it means to love and respect other people.

By taking the advice from this chapter and the next, we can become better parents—and better teachers in our home school. We've laid the foundation by nurturing the balance between our ME and WE, and we've added the building blocks of shared parenting and empathetic discipline. Together these elements create a warm environment to nurture our children in a caring parent-child relationship. Such an environment will help ensure a smooth transition through the teenage years. More than anything else, what is related to adolescent well-being is having parents who are emotionally available to them. A relationship like that begins when the children are young. The next chapter summarizes strategies that strengthen marriages and improve parenting.

Chapter 9

Winning Strategies

Tips for Expectant and New Parents

Many of the parents groaned when I asked them if they had any advice for new or expectant parents. They said things like, "Everyone gives you advice." Even so, they realized that new parents NEED a lot of advice. Likely you've thought of the many benefits that come from having children. Therefore, the tips below focus on what people are less likely to consider as they think about becoming parents.

Tips for Those Thinking about Having Children

1. Get A Life!

As much as possible, get your personal "ego" needs met before the first child comes along. Children take most of your time, attention, and money. They need to be the focus of your life while they are young. Having your own education completed, your career begun and some types of adventures satisfied before you have kids frees you to enjoy them completely and be the best parent you can be. Not surprisingly, it is much easier to complete your college education or graduate degree before you have to be thinking about finding childcare and paying for diapers. A good time to have children comes when you've settled into your new career with at least a year's experience. Several couples in my study actually changed careers once or twice after the birth of their children, putting incredible strain on the family system.

Also consider that many types of vacations are not feasible with young children, either because of the expense or because it's not the kind of things kids like to do. If the kids aren't having a good time, you won't be either. Disney World will be more fun if you're not wishing you'd made that wine tasting tour in the Sonoma Valley. My husband and I refer to the family reunion we went to when our twins were one year old as "a week of childcare in the mountains." You'll have to put off that romp through Europe for years.

2. Get a Grip on Your Finances.

As wonderful as children are, we have to realize that children are expensive. It costs more to raise a child to age 18, before college, than to buy your house and two cars combined![44] Be smart about it. You wouldn't buy a house or a car you couldn't afford, would you? So don't start making financial mistakes with life's most precious asset. Indeed, children are a gift from God but God expects us to be good stewards with our children and with our finances. Try to have no debt when you have a child. Financial strains are very taxing on a marriage and you want your little bundle to be a bundle of joy rather than a bundle of high interest payments. Plan ahead. Live frugally. Ways to cut down on expenses and reduce debt include eating at home, getting rid of satellite TV and gas guzzling vehicles, and using pay-as-you-go cell phones like TracFone and Virgin Mobile rather than paying over forty dollars a month for cell phone service. Use the money saved to pay off any debts you may have: Credit cards, school loans, even your house. Did you realize that if you buy a house on a 20-year loan at 8 percent you'll pay more in interest than you did for the house? Pay it off sooner and save a fortune—a fortune that can go to your child's college savings account.

In light of America's spending patterns, this point may seem extreme but what kind of expert would I be if I didn't tell you the truth? If I were an expert on health would you respect my advice if I said, "A little obesity is okay"? So while this point may sound harsh, it's not nearly as harsh as indebtedness. And, as long as I'm laying on the bad news, financial problems are directly related to divorce.

3. Beware: We hear what we want to hear.

If you've decided you want kids, you've probably started filtering out the problems people tell you about. But when people tell you about all the blessings of parenthood, THEN you pay attention! (By the way, did you pay attention to points one and two?) Listen when people complain about having children. This will help you be less surprised when you're confronted with these difficulties yourself.

4. Get Some Practice.

Volunteer to take care of infants. (Yes, guys, this tip is for you too!) Start by asking family and friends if you can hold their babies. Then lengthen the amount of time you're in charge. Your church nursery is a good place to get some experience. You only have to do it for an hour or two at a time, and make sure you're there with someone skilled with babies. Getting some practice will give you more confidence for when you have your own—24/7.

5. Get Equity.

"Bear one another's burdens and thus fulfill the law of Christ" (Gal. 3:28). Divide tasks, chores, and decision-making responsibilities according to a fair distribution of time and (un)pleasantness rather than blindly following gendered stereotypes of responsibilities. Sometimes people do things based on "the way I was raised" without considering the consequences of this process. By thinking through responsibilities, the two of you can work things so that you're doing the chores you hate least and you can make sure that neither of you is overburdened.

Your relationship and how you divide tasks with your spouse is uniquely yours. Therefore, you need to grant yourselves permission to do things the way that suits your unique situation. Agree to have the courage to please yourselves instead of bowing to the pressures sometimes felt from extended family, church, and friends.

It's important to do this before you have kids because once people have kids, they tend to fall back into old patterns which are often gender stereotyped and can leave one or both parents feeling overburdened and resentful.

Tips for Those Expecting Their First Child

6. Identify Your Expectations.

Use the questions in the next chapter to identify your expectations and then read the introduction to this book as well as Chapters 1, 2, and 3 to reflect on what kind of parent you want to be and how to take care of your ME-WE-ME.

7. Talk to Each Other.

Sounds simple, doesn't it? You'll notice that the interview questions for expectant parents in Chapter 10 repeatedly ask, "Did you talk about that or was it assumed?" It's amazing how often we just assume our spouse thinks the same way we do.

I interviewed wives and husbands separately and they sometimes disagreed—one couple didn't even agree about whether the baby was planned or not. With another couple both expected to take the child to childcare—that's a happy accident, but what if both assumed the other parent would be taking her? People were more likely to have worked out job details like: Who will work when? Who will take care of the child while each of you works? How will you split sick days when the child is sick or some other activity comes up?

There are many, many details that need to be discussed even though they will need to be renegotiated later. For instance, how will you handle getting up during the night? If mom is doing all of the night-feedings, how will dad even out the score? How will you divide diapers? Washing baby clothes? Baths?

How will you take care of your WE as a couple once you have a child?

8. Discuss Your Roles.

One specific topic to talk to each other about is how you envision your role as a parent and also how you envision your spouse's role as a parent. Similar to those unrealized expectations about how our vacation destination will look, we have expectations about ourselves and our spouse that we often take for granted. In order to uncover your and your spouse's assumptions, sit down and take turns talking about how you saw your own mother as a mother. What did you like about it? What do you want to do differently? Do the same about your father.

9. Work on Your Conflicts Now.

Your life is about to get more complicated. Smooth the path for your new baby as much as possible by working through the marital conflicts you've built up over time. They always happen; it doesn't mean anything is wrong with your marriage. The only thing that would be wrong would be to deny you have conflicts and not work on them.

10. Realize That Your Family Is Going to Affect Your Work.

There are going to be days when you really need to get stuff done at work but your child is sick and for one reason or another, your spouse can't help. There may be job opportunities that would require your happily located family to move, so you will put your family first and say "no" to career gains. In fact, if a parent doesn't recognize that family affects his/her work, that parent is probably over-investing in work at his/her family's expense.

For more on this, read Chapter 6 on Work.

11. Develop a Childcare Plan.

Whether both parents are working full time, one parent is staying at home or everything in between, spend some time working out a plan for childcare. For working parents, this includes interviewing potential providers and getting on waiting lists.

All couples need to schedule specific times when one parent will be "off" and the other parent will be responsible for childcare. For instance, mom may be off on Tuesday nights from 6:00-9:00 and dad is off on Thursday nights from 6:00-9:00. Such a plan doesn't mean that the parent who is off-duty can't be home, it just means there are three hours a week when you don't have to be responsible for the child. This need for specific times off is particularly necessary for stay-at-home moms. They tend to think of childcare as their full-time jobs and while this is the case, a full-time job rarely runs more than eighty hours a week. But full-time childcare is 24/7, making it a 168-hour work week!

See Chapter 6 for more about planning for childcare.

Tips for Parents

12. Manage Your Life Well.

When parents don't manage their own lives well, the effects ripple through the rest of the family. For example, when one parent doesn't take care of things until the last minute or always runs late, the spouse and the children are affected, often with increased feelings of stress. The reverse is true too: When parents manage their own lives well, everyone in the family system is more stable, secure, and happy.

13. Take Care of Your WE as a Couple.

As Norm says,

Number one, make sure you still take time for just you and your spouse because after your children are grown, then it'll be just the couple left and they need to know each other.

That's not the only reason: It's common for couples' marital satisfaction to drop while they are raising kids, partly because they get so focused on being good parents that they neglect their relationship with each other. Your kids benefit from their parents enjoying each other.

Answer the questions for parents in Chapter 10 and then read Chapter 4, "Rebalancing the ME-WE-ME."

14. Revisit the Decisions You Made Before the Baby Was Born and Talk About Them Again Once the Baby Arrives.

Some of the parents in my study thought they had good plans for how they were sharing responsibilities but when they actually started living out these plans, unexpected negative effects arose. Diane and Derek learned this lesson through trial and error. When Andrea was born, Diane thought she could do it all. She was a stay-at-home mom, so she thought it was reasonable for her to meet Andrea's every need. Before long, she had conditioned Andrea to only want her and Derek was left out of the picture. When their second child came along, Diane and Derek made sure to have Derek involved from the get-go so that the baby would be satisfied with either parent. This likely helps explain why their second baby is easier-going.

Unfortunately, Elyse's story doesn't have the happy ending. From the beginning Elyse figured she'd have to do it all herself. She never even tried negotiating with Edward, and sadly, Edward didn't take on any of the parenting duties himself. Exhausted now and with two young children, Elyse feels like the pattern has been set for so long that there's no undoing it—except through divorce and, obviously, that's not going to get Edward more involved. No doubt she'd like Edward to adopt Sid's perspective:

> *Even after four years, there are still responsibilities when you come home. You just can't go, "Okay, the day's over with and I'm done." When you come home you've got to be able to focus on the family. They need your attention probably more than anybody at work does.*

15. Pay Attention to How Your Family Has to Sacrifice for Your Work.

There's a give-and-take between work and family, a *quid pro quo*. They need each other. Your family needs your work to pay the bills and to give you outside interests. And your work needs your family to attend to your physical and emotional needs so that you stay a productive worker. But don't fool yourself into thinking that your work doesn't take a toll on your family. The biggest typical problems are when you work too many hours or require your family to move. Of course, your family needs your income, but occasionally ask yourself: "Do

I have a choice to make a little less income in order to have more time and more stability for my family?"

Illustrating this point, Chris Rock described how he sought to stay home with his daughters as much as possible. To emphasize his position, he said, "I don't want my daughter to see my movie and say, 'You weren't at my recital for that piece of *&%#?!'[45]

16. Work as a Team.

Since people so often think of parenting and family as women's domains, men sometimes don't feel like they're much needed in the nurturance department. People often assume that mothers "naturally" know how to mother, but actually they usually learn how to do it because all the messages around them tell them they have to. While this can seem like a bonus to man, allowing him to relax after a hard day's work, it can also leave him feeling like he's pushed out of the picture and like he's mostly needed as a money machine.

A simple change in framing can help make men embrace their importance in the family—think of your family as a team. When mothers and fathers work as a team, both learning to parent at the same time with that newborn, they win at least two ways: 1) They have an empathetic teammate when the going gets rough; and 2) They avoid that good parent/lesser parent setup so many couples used to have. Just listen to the wisdom of Ecclesiastes 4:9-11. "[9] Two people are better off than one, for they can help each other succeed. [10] If one person falls, the other can reach out and help. But someone who falls alone is in real trouble. [11] Likewise, two people lying close together can keep each other warm. But how can one be warm alone?"

Read more about working as a team in Chapter 8.

17. Guys, Stay in the Game!

Guys, imagine you and your wife are on a community volleyball team. She's a better player than you and she says, "Just move out of the way and I'll take the shots." Likely, you wouldn't be willing to just step out of the way and let her play while you look on and occasionally cheer her on. That certainly wouldn't improve your volleyball skills and, after a while, you might not feel like you have much of a place on the team.

Fallon, whose husband is truly a team player, gives this advice with gratitude about her own situation:

> *If the marriage has been that the female has done the lion's share of the housework, that's going to have to change. The man's going to have to step in and help out because you just can't do it all, even if she's a stay-at-home mom."*

For more on this, read Chapter 5, "Winning Teams."

18. Women, Move out of the Way!

Continuing with the volleyball game illustration, a good teammate helps her partner by allowing him to get some practice and develop his own style. If you just take over and hog the ball (or the baby), you keep the team from being the best it can be. Chapter 8, "Every Home Is a Home School," describes how to maximize all of your team players' potentials.

19. Think in Terms of the Whole Family System.

As a team, you and your spouse are stronger than you are apart and, together, you can take care of the paid work, childcare, and housework. As Jesus said, "If a house is divided against itself, that house will not be able to stand" (Mark 3:25). As the kids get older, they increasingly become part of the team, all working together to get family needs met and all being strengthened to go out and face the world. Chapter 8 describes how to discipline children in a way that develops them into good team players.

20. Don't Be in Denial About Sleep Deprivation.

When Christopher and I had newborn twins, we were surprised that people weren't more considerate of nap time and early bedtimes. The phone would ring after 9:00 in the evening and we would be livid! In our sleep-deprived states, we didn't even think to turn off the phone ringer and disconnect the doorbell. (Our motto was, "Never wake a sleeping baby.") Quite a few of the expectant parents in my study realized that they would be getting less sleep. That's a good realization to have, but make plans to deal with sleep deprivation before the baby arrives. Once she's home, you'll be trying to decode those cries and at least one of you won't be making the best of decisions precisely because you're sleep-deprived.

21. Let It Go.

The couples I studied who had stable marriages and careers before their first babies were born seemed to be the most surprised with how much having children had turned their lives upside down. As Frank put it:

Relax, and don't say, 'Well, my kids will never do that.' I've seen people in church with their kids running around like a bunch of wild Indians. And I've said, 'My kids are not going to do that. My kids will never be in my bed with me. My kids . . .' Never say, 'Never,' because I've had three in bed with me at one time. I've got one in bed with me right now, every night. My kids run around like wild Indians. I used to always say, 'My kids will never do that.' Yeah, your kids will.

Walls can be repainted, and you won't be driving the same car forever, so when they rip a hole in the seat, or they run the tricycle into the side of the car and put a big dent in it, it's just a car Just relax and don't worry about it. I mean 10 years from now, you're not gonna remember that crayon on the wall. Don't sweat the small stuff.

22. Read, read, read.

Reading was a popular response to what advice people wanted to pass on to expectant and new parents. Having a baby is indescribably meaningful and rewarding. It's also one of the most disruptive of life's events. Consequently, information is your friend. Get as much of it as you can. While books can't tell you everything, they do tell you something.

23. Be Flexible

Even though Adam was one of the many who suggested reading, he added,

Be flexible. It's very difficult to plan because you never know if they're going to be sick, you never know what activities they may need to do. You try to plan around things but there are so many things that are unknown. If you go in saying, 'This is the way it's going to be' and you're not willing to make changes in your current activities, there's going to be a lot of conflict.

24. Get Help.

Sometimes parents—especially mothers—think that they need to do all of the childcare themselves in order to be a good parent. However, that's just not true. All through human history children have been cared for routinely by a variety of involved adults, not just one or two. The prevalence of many adults helping in childcare in tribal cultures is conveyed in the African proverb, "It takes a village to raise a child." Parents and children alike benefit from an extended network of people who participate in the children's care and nurturance. Quite a few of the parents I studied were lucky enough to have one or both sets of grandparents living nearby and everyone had used Mother's Day Out at churches at one time or another (though some of the stay-at-home moms were reluctant to admit this!).

25. Resolve Conflicts Left Over from the First Baby Before You Have a Second One.

Having two children is harder and takes up more of your time than having one. Those unresolved conflicts could send you over the edge. As they say in Texas, "If you find yourself in a hole, stop digging." Resolving deep-seated conflicts isn't easy. Look to Chapter 8 for suggestions.

Chapter 10

Check it out
for Yourself

Many of the people in this study commented on the fact that the actual process of answering the survey and interview questions helped them clarify some of their own expectations. It also helped them discuss the issues with their spouses.

Realizing that we have choices and purposefully thinking through issues helps us all to have the best families we can have—families that nurture the growth and happiness of each of their members.

Consequently, the survey and interview questions are provided in this chapter so that others can use them in clarifying and discussing their own expectations as they embark into the world of parenthood. This chapter is divided into three sections: 1) Questions for first time expectant mothers, 2) Questions for first time expectant fathers, 3) Questions for mothers and fathers with children. The end of each section includes tables reporting on the mothers and fathers in this study.

Expectant Mothers

Survey of First Time, Expectant Mothers[46]

1. Will this be your first child?
2. Are you living with the child's father?
3. What is your marital status?
4. Age _____

Please answer from 1—strongly disagree to 5—strongly agree with 3 being neutral.

_____5. I had a career before I became pregnant.
_____6. My pay is essential to my family.
_____7. My professional advancement is important to me.
_____8. I put a lot of investment into my job training before becoming pregnant.
_____9. I was established in my career before becoming pregnant.
____10. My income will allow me to pay for quality childcare while I work.
____11. There are good incentives to return to work after becoming a mother.
____12. A mother's role is to prioritize her family over career/work.
____13. A father's role is to prioritize his family over career/work.
____14. Children suffer from not having a full-time, stay at home mom.
____15. My husband and I have discussed how we will share responsibilities for child care (changing diapers, feeding, taking off from work when the child is sick, etc.)

_____16. A father and mother should split child care responsibilities equally.

_____17. After our child is born, my husband would prefer for me to work.

Please answer the following using 1—very negative to 5—very positive with 3 being neutral.

_____18. Maternal employment has a _____ impact on children's well-being.

_____19. Maternal employment has a _____ impact on children's performance in school.

_____20. Maternal employment has a _____ effect on children's cognitive development.

_____21. Maternal employment has a _____ effect on children's emotional development.

22. Average number of employed hours worked per week before pregnancy:_____

23. Average number of employed hours you expect to work per week once your child is six months old: _____

24. I expect to begin working at least 20 hours/week by the time my youngest child is age _____. (Write NA if you never intend to work 20 hours/week).

25. I expect to begin working at least 40 hours/week by the time my youngest child is age _____. (Write NA if you never intend to work 40 hours/week).

26. Highest level of education completed: _____

27. Family Income (before taxes): $_____ per (circle one) week, month, year

Please answer from 1—strongly disagree to 5—strongly agree with 3 being neutral.

_____28. I am concerned about finding dependable childcare.

_____29. I would prefer not to work but am forced to by financial pressure.

_____30. My job is emotionally satisfying.

_____31. I feel that my pregnancy has had a negative effect on my job security.

_____32. I feel that being a mother will have a negative effect on my job security.

_____33. I enjoy going to work.

_____34. My job is boring.

_____35. I feel that my job serves an important purpose.

_____36. My job does not have much meaning for me.

_____37. I dread going to work.

_____38. My work is likely to significantly affect the lives of other people.

39. Please comment on how you and your husband intend to share work and child care responsibilities.

Table 1:
Expectant Mothers' Characteristics and Attitudes

	Mean
Aspects of Career	
Had career before pregnancy	3.46
Established in career	3.13
Investment in job training	3.43
Importance of advancement	3.60
Pregnancy has affected job security negatively	1.97
Motherhood will affect job security negatively	1.95
Number of Work Hours	
Average hours worked before pregnancy	31-40/week
Hours expects to work when child is 6 months old	15-25/week
Hours expects to work when youngest child in first grade	25-35/week
Job Satisfaction	
Job is emotionally satisfying	3.38
Enjoys going to work	3.49
Feels job serves important purpose	3.81
Feels kind of work affects lives of others	3.42
Job is boring (r)	2.03
Job does not have much meaning (r)	2.36
Dreads going to work (r)	2.23
Financial	
Annual family income	33,857.66
Pay is essential to my family	3.46
Income allows for quality childcare	2.90
Good incentives for returning to work	3.32
Prefer not to work, but must for financial reasons	3.12
Effects of Mother Working	
Children suffer when mom does not stay home	2.89
Impact of mother's employment on child's well-being	3.13
Impact of mother's employment on child's schoolwork	3.26
Impact of mother's employment on child's cognitive dev.	3.18
Impact of mother's employment on child's emotional dev.	3.10
Childcare	
Concerned about finding dependable childcare	3.87
Have discussed with husband how will share childcare	4.03
Husband's Attitude	
Husband prefers wife to work after baby is born	2.62
Gender Attitudes	
If both parents work full-time, childcare split equally	4.08
If both parents work full-time, housework split equally	4.24
If wife returns to work housework will be mostly hers	2.85
Mother's role is to put family first	3.98
Father's role is to put family first	3.87
Demographics	
Marital status	Married
Age	23.26
Level of education	some college
Race	86% White
	14% Hispanic

Responses were on a five point scale with 5 being highest, 3 being neutral and 1 being the lowest rating.
N=63

Table 2:
How a Mother's Employment Will Affect Her Child's School Performance,
Cognitive Development, and Emotional Development According to the Mother

	Negative Effect	No Effect	Positive Effect
Child's Well Being	19.4%	50%	30.6%
Child's Performance	11.3%	53.2%	35.5%
Child's Cognitive Development	11.3%	61.3%	27.4%
Child's Emotional Development	17.7%	56.5%	25.8%

Responses were on a five point scale with 5 being highest, 3 being neutral and 1 being the lowest rating.
N=63

Expectant Mothers' Interview Questions

Age_____
How long you have been in your current relationship?
Are you married or cohabiting?
When are you planning to have a child or children?
How many?

Answer all questions in the sections relevant to your situation.

SECTION A

1. Do you work full-time, part-time or stay at home?
2. Did your mother work? How did you feel about that? (How old were you and your siblings when she went back to work? Was the income helpful?)
3. If you could arrange things just the way you want-ed, what would you prefer to be doing right now: Working at your present job, working at another job or not working at all?
4. Why? (if working at home, skip to section B)
5. If working for pay, what type of industry/business do you work for?
6. What type of work do you do?

7. What are your main duties?
8. About how many hours do you usually work in a week?
9. Is that a 9 to 5 schedule? If not, please describe.
10. How long have you been working at that job/in that line of work?
11. On the whole, would you say that your job is really interesting, just okay or boring? Why?
12. What are the things you like most about your job?
13. What are the things you dislike most about your job?
14. What are the main reasons you are working now?
15. Different people want different things out of their jobs. What are the things you feel are most important in a job?

Why? (ideas to consider: Advancement, people you work with, type of work, pay, amount of independence, amount of prestige)

16. Has working affected your feelings about yourself in any way?
17. Do you intend to work full-time, part-time or stay at home once your child is born?
18. How did you arrive at this decision?
    How does your husband feel about this decision?
19. Imagine for a moment that you were (not) going to work once your child was born. How would you feel about that?

Do you think your mental outlook would be better or worse if you were not working? (Assume you could afford not to work.)

Section B (for respondents who are not working)

20. Have you worked in the past? (if no, go to b.)
21. What type of work did you do?
22. How did you feel about your work?

23. Why did you stop working?
24. Do you think not working has affected your feelings about yourself in any way?
25. Have you ever thought about going (back) to work?
26. How does your husband feel about your not working?
27. Imagine for a moment that you had a full-time job. How do you think that would affect your life?

Do you think your mental outlook would be better or worse if you were working?

Section C (for everyone)

28. Do you think having a child will affect your life in general?
29. How do you think your life will be different once your child is born?
30. Do you think your mental outlook will be better or worse?

Your feelings about yourself?

31. Was your child planned? (if no skip to 33)
32. If so, why did you choose to have a child at this time?
33. Was work a factor in your decision to have a child?
34. Are breadwinning responsibilities split 50-50? If not, who is the primary breadwinner?
35. How do you and your husband split housework?
How do you feel about that?
36. Have you and your husband talked about how you will share child care?
How will you and your husband be sharing work, housework and child care once your child is born?
37. Comment on how your family or friends have influenced your decision making regarding work and family.
How do you feel about that?

Section D (for mothers who plan to continue working)

38. How do you think having children will affect your
    plans for work?
Do you think raising children will affect with your ability to work outside your home or pursue a career?
39. Do you think working outside the home will affect
    with your ability to raise a family?
Will it involve any sacrifices for you or your family?
40. Will work sacrifices be shared? Equally?
41. Did you decide together? Assumed?
42. What if your husband wanted you not to work?
    (Assuming you had enough money)

Section E (for mothers who plan to stay at home)

43. What are the main reasons you plan to devote most
    of your time to raising a family and not working?
44. Are considerations of your children a factor in your
    decision not to work?
45. Will you have to give up anything important in or-
    der to raise a family?
46. Is there anything about not working or pursuing a
    career that bothers you?
47. Do you want a career? Why (not)?
48. Has there ever been a time when you didn't want to
    have children or did want to have a career?
49. Why (not)?
50. What if your husband wanted you to work?
51. If respondent plans to go to work eventually: What
    do you think you will do when you return to work?
How do you think stopping work will affect your chances
of finding the kind of job you want?

Section F (for everyone)

52. Do you anticipate any problems with sharing child care with your husband?
How might you resolve them?
53. Are you currently planning to have any more children?
If yes, how many?
54. How definite are your plans?
55. What are your main reasons for (not) having another child?
56. Any closing comments?

Expectant Fathers

Survey of First Time, Expectant Fathers

1. Will this be your first child? (circle one)
2. Are you living with the child's mother? (circle one)
3. What is your marital status? _____
4. Age _____

Please answer from 1—strongly disagree to 5—strongly agree with 3 being neutral.

____5. I wish my father had spent more time with me while I was growing up.
____6. My pay is essential to my family.
____7. My professional advancement is important to me.
____8. I have invested a lot into my job training.
____9. My income will allow me to pay for quality child-care while I work.

_____10. My wife and I have discussed how we will share responsibilities for child- care (changing diapers, feeding, taking off from work when the child is sick, etc.)

_____11. If a father and mother both work full time, they should split childcare responsibilities equally.

_____12. If a father and mother both work full time, they should split housework equally.

_____13. After our child is born, I would prefer my wife to work.

_____14. If both my wife and I work full-time, the housework will be mostly up to me.

_____15. I am concerned about finding dependable childcare.

_____16. My job is emotionally satisfying.

_____17. I feel that being a father will have a negative effect on my job security.

_____18. I enjoy going to work.

_____19. My job is boring.

_____20. I feel that my job serves an important purpose.

_____21. The kind of work I do is likely to significantly affect the lives of other people.

_____22. A mother's role is to prioritize her family over career/work.

_____23. A father's role is to prioritize his family over career/work.

_____24. Children suffer from not having a full-time, stay at home mom.

25. Average number of employed hours worked per week before your wife's pregnancy: _____

26. Average number of employed hours you expect to work per week once your child is six months old:

_____

27. Highest level of education completed: _____

28. Family income (before taxes): $_____
    per (circle one) week, month, year

If you are not employed, skip to question #32.

29. How much time do you plan to take off after your child is born?

30. Does your company offer any kind of family-supportive programs?
(eg: subsidized childcare, flex-time, other alternative work schedules)

31. If you answered yes on #30, do you plan to take advantage of any or all of these programs? _____ No _____ Yes (please name which ones)

32. What is your city/town of residence? _____

33. What is your race/ethnicity? _____

Please answer the following using 1—very negative to 5—very positive with 3 being neutral.

34. A mother's employment has a _____ impact on children's well-being.

35. A mother's employment has a _____ impact on children's performance in school.

36. A mother's employment has a _____ effect on children's cognitive development.

37. A mother's employment has a _____ effect on children's emotional development.

39. Please comment on how you and your wife intend to share work and childcare responsibilities. (Use the back of this sheet if necessary).

Table 3:
Expectant Fathers' Attitudes and Characteristics

	Mean
Work Orientation	
Advancement is important to me	4.04
Invested a lot in job training	3.64
Job is emotionally satisfying	3.50
Fatherhood will have negative effect on job	1.60
Enjoys going to work	3.96
Job is boring	1.84
Feels job serves important purpose	4.40
Kind of work affects lives of other people	4.08
My pay is essential to my family	4.29
Attitudes Regarding Childcare	
Have discussed sharing childcare with wife	3.92
Wish father spent more time with me	2.96
My income will pay for childcare	3.20
Both parents work full-time, childcare shared equally	4.00
Concerned about finding childcare	3.36
Job offers family supportive programs	1.43
Will use job related family support programs	1.63
Attitudes Regarding Housework	
Both parents work full-time, housework shared equally	4.08
Both parents work full-time, housework up to me	2.28
Gender Roles	
After child's birth, prefers wife to work	2.52
Mother's role is to put family first	3.84
Father's role is to put family first	3.92
Demographics	
Marital status	married
Age	26.96
Level of education	some college
Household income	39,450.53
Days of planned time off after baby is born	7.6
White, non-Hispanic	86%
Hispanic	14%

Responses were on a five point scale with 5 being highest, 3 being neutral and
1 being the lowest rating.

N=25

Table 4:
Expectant Father's Attitude Regarding How a Mother's Employment Will Affect Her Child's School Performance, Cognitive Development, and Emotional Development

	Negative Effect	No Effect	Positive Effect
Child's Well Being	20%	48%	32%
Child's Performance	24.%	56%	16%
Child's Cognitive Development	8%	72%	16%
Child's Emotional Development	24%	60%	16%

N=25

Expectant Fathers' Interview Questions

Age_____
How long you have been in your current relationship?
Are you married or cohabiting?
When are you planning to have a child or children?
How many?

Answer all questions in the sections relevant to your situation.

<u>Section A</u>

1. Did your mother work? How did you feel about that? (How old were you and your siblings when she went back to work? Was the income helpful?
2. What is your occupational status?
3. If working for pay, what type of industry/business do you work for?
4. If you could arrange things just the way you wanted, what would you prefer to be doing right now? Working at your present job, working at another job or not working at all?
5. Why? (if not working, skip to section B)
6. What type of work do you do?

7. What are your main duties?
8. About how many hours do you usually work in a week?
9. Is that a 9 to 5 schedule? If not, please describe.
10. Has working affected your feelings about yourself in any way?
11. Do you intend to work more, less, or the same once your child is born?
    How did you arrive at this decision?   How does your wife feel about this decision?)
12. Do you plan to take parental leave?
    How did you arrive at this decision?   How does your wife feel about this decision?)
13. Imagine for a moment that you were not going to work once your child was born. How would you feel about that?   (Assume you could afford not to work – eg. wife was working.)

Do you think your mental outlook would be better or worse if you were not working?

Section B (for respondents who are not working)

14. Have you worked in the past? (if no, go to b.)
15. What type of work did you do?
16. How did you feel about your work?
17. Why did you stop working?
18. Do you think not working has affected your feelings about yourself in any way?
19. Have you ever thought about going (back) to work?
20. How does your wife feel about your not working?
21. Imagine for a moment that you had a full-time job. How do you think that would affect your life?

(Probe: Do you think your mental outlook would be better or worse if you were working?)

Section C (for everyone)

22. What does fatherhood mean to you?
(Eg: Parenting roles, responsibilities, duties, etc.)
23. Do you feel that the sex of your child will affect how much quality time you spend with him/her?
24. Do you feel that it would be easier to raise a boy or a girl?
25. Do you think your attitudes about paternal child-care responsibilities differ from your own father's? Please explain (what were his attitudes).
26. How do you feel about a father who has reduced his hours at work in favor of home activities?
27. Do you think having a child will affect your life in general?
Your feelings about yourself?
28. How do you think your life will be different once your child is born?
Do you think your mental outlook will be better or worse? What about time for hobbies, sports, etc.?
29. Have you and your wife talked about how you will share childcare?
If you both work full time, who will be responsible for arranging childcare?
30. If you and the baby's mother are both employed full time, whose responsibility will it be to make last minute arrangements which could mean taking time off work?
(For example, if your child care provider were to cancel at the last minute or if the child was too ill to leave with the regular care provider?
31. Do you anticipate any problems with sharing child-care with your wife?
How might you resolve any problems that could come up?
32. Was your child planned? (If no skip to #35)
33. If so, why did you choose to have a child at this time?

34. Was work a factor in your decision to have a child?
(Probe: Did you take into consideration your earnings, time spent at work, etc.?)

35. Are breadwinning responsibilities split 50-50? If not, who is the primary breadwinner?

36. Will your wife be working after the child is born? Full time/ part time?
(Probe: How do you feel about that?)

37. How do you and your wife split housework?
(Probe: How do you feel about that?)

38. What types of household chores are your responsibility?
Will that change after the child is born? How?

39. Comment on how your family and friends have influenced your decision making regarding work and family. How do you feel about that?

Section D (for fathers who plan to continue working)

40. How do you think having children will affect your work? Do you think raising children will affect your ability to pursue a career?)

41. Do you think working will involve any sacrifices for you or your family?

42. ill work sacrifices be shared? Equally?

43. Did you decide together? Assumed?

Section E (for fathers who plan to stay at home)

44. What are the main reasons you plan to devote most of your time to raising a family rather than outside employment?
(Probe: Benefits of having children and costs of working)

45. Are considerations of your children a factor in your decision not to work?

46. Will you have to give up anything important in order to stay at home and raise a family?
    Is there anything about not working or pursuing a career that bothers you?
47. Do you want a career? Why (not)?
48. What if your wife wanted you to work?
49. Do you plan to go to work eventually?
    What do you think you will do when you return to work?

How do you think stopping work will affect your chances of finding the kind of job you want?

<u>Section F (for everyone)</u>

50. Are you currently planning to have any more children?
    If yes, how many?
51. How definite are your plans?
52. What are your main reasons for (not) having another child?
53. Any closing comments?

Survey of Mothers

1. How many children do you have?_____
   What are their ages? _____
2. Are you living with your child(ren)'s father?
3. Marital Status: _____
4. Age _____

Please answer from 1—strongly disagree to 5—strongly agree with 3 being neutral.

_____ 5. I had a career before I became pregnant.
_____ 6. My pay is essential to my family.

_____ 7. My professional advancement is important to me.

_____ 8. My income allows me to pay for quality child-care while I work.

_____ 9. A mother's role is to prioritize her family over career/work.

_____10. A father's role is to prioritize his family over career/work.

_____11. If a father and mother both work full time, they should split childcare responsibilities equally.

_____12. If a father and mother both work full time, they should split housework equally.

_____13. My husband prefers me to work.

14. Please give an estimate of how your husband and you share responsibilities for child care (changing diapers, feeding, taking off from work when the child is sick, etc.) Example: You 50%, him 50% or you 75%, him 25%
(Your response should total 100%).

Please answer the following using 1—very negative to 5—very positive with 3 being neutral.

_____15. Maternal employment has a _____ impact on children's well-being.

_____16. Maternal employment has a _____ impact on children's performance in school.

_____17. Maternal employment has a_____ effect on children's cognitive development.

_____18. Maternal employment has a _____ effect on children's emotional development.

19. Average number of employed hours worked per week before your first child: _____

20. Average number of employed hours you work per week now: _____

21. Average number of employed hours per week your husband worked before your first child:_____

22. Average number of employed hours your husband works per week now: _____

23. Highest level of education completed: _____

24. Family Income (before taxes): $_____ per (circle one) week, month, year

25. What is your city/town of residence? _____

26. What is your race/ethnicity? _____ /

For Employed Mothers: (If staying at home full time, please skip this section).

Please answer from 1—strongly disagree to 5—strongly agree with 3 being neutral.

____27. I have dependable childcare.

____28. I would prefer not to work but am forced to by financial pressure.

____29. My job is emotionally satisfying.

____30. Being a mother has a negative effect on my job security.

____31. I feel that my job serves an important purpose.

32. How much time did you take off after each of your children were born?

33. Does your company offer any kind of family-supportive programs?

(eg: subsidized childcare, flex-time, other alternative work schedules)

   _____ No _____ Yes

34. If you answered yes on #33, do you take advantage of any or all of these programs?_____ No _____ Yes (please name which ones)

Table 5:
Mothers' Attitudes toward Work and Home

	Mean
Career	
Had career before pregnancy	4.29
Importance of advancement	3.00
Number of Work Hours	
Average hours worked before first child	38.93
Average hours you work now	22.71
Average hours husband worked before first child	42.50
Average hours husband works now	51.29
Financial Needs	
Your income (includes stay-at-home moms)	14,117.14
Your husband's income	42,538.57
My pay is essential to my family	3.07
My income allows for quality childcare	3.00
Effects of Mother Working	
Impact of mother's employment on child's well-being	3.57
Impact of mother's employment on child's schoolwork	3.43
Impact of mother's employment on child's cognitive dev.	3.50
Impact of mother's employment on child's emotional dev.	3.50
Husband's Attitude	
Husband prefers wife to work	2.62
Gender Attitudes	
If both parents work full-time, childcare split equally	4.50
If both parents work full-time, housework split equally	4.57
What percentage of childcare are you doing	71.79
What percentage of childcare is your husband doing	28.21
Father's role is to put family first	4.36
Mother's role is to put family first	4.50
Employed Mothers	
I have dependable childcare	4.71
Prefer not to work, but must for financial reasons	3.29
Job is emotionally satisfying	3.71
Motherhood affects job security negatively	1.71
Feels job serves important purpose	4.14
Amount of time taken off for first child	48.83 days
Amount of time taken off for second child	40.75 days
Company offers family supportive programs	1.29
Takes advantage of these programs	2.00
Employed mothers income	28,234.29
Demographics	
How many children do you have	2.14
Age of first child	58.00 months
Age of second child	29.91 months
Age of third child	13.00 months
Number of years you have been married	8.89
Age	31.36
Level of education	Some college
Race	93% white, non-Hisp
	7% Hispanic

Responses were on a five point scale with 5 being highest, 3 being neutral and
1 being the lowest rating.
N=14

Table 6:
How a Mother's Employment Will Affect Her Child's School Performance,
Cognitive Development, and Emotional Development According to the Mother

	Negative Effect	No Effect	Positive Effect
Child's Well Being	7.1%	42.9%	50.0%
Child's Performance	7.1%	57.1%	35.7%
Child's Cognitive Development	14.3%	35.7%	50.0%
Child's Emotional Development	21.4%	21.4%	57.1%

N=14

Survey of Fathers

1. How many children do you have?_____
        What are their ages? _____
2. Are you living with the child(ren)'s mother? _____
3. Marital Status: _____
4. Age _____

Please answer from 1—strongly disagree to 5—strongly agree with 3 being neutral.

_____5. I wish my father had spent more time with me while I was growing up.

_____6. My pay is essential to my family.

_____7. My professional advancement is important to me.

_____8. My income allows me to pay for quality child-care while I work.

_____9. A father's role is to prioritize his family over career/work.

___10. A mother's role is to prioritize her family over career/work.

___11. If a father and mother both work full time, they should split childcare responsibilities equally.

_____12. If a father and mother both work full time, they should split housework equally.

_____13. I prefer for my wife to work.

14. Please give an estimate of how you and your wife share responsibilities for child care (changing diapers, feeding, taking off from work when the child is sick, etc.) Example: You 50%, her 50% or you 75%, her 25%

(Your response should total 100%).

15. Average number of employed hours worked per week before your first child:_____

16. Average number of employed hours you work per week now: _____

17. Average number of employed hours worked per week your wife worked before your first child: _____

18. Average number of employed hours your wife works per week now: _____

19. Highest level of education completed:_____

20. Family income (before taxes): $_____ per (circle one) week, month, year

21. What is your city/town of residence?_____

22. What is your race/ethnicity? _____

23. How much time did you take off after each of your children were born?

Please answer the following using 1—very negative to 5—very positive with 3 being neutral.

24. A mother's employment has a _____ impact on children's well-being.

25. A mother's employment has a _____ impact on children's performance in school.

26. A mother's employment has a _____ effect on children's cognitive development.

27. A mother's employment has a _____ effect on children's emotional development.

For Employed Fathers: (If staying at home full time, please skip this section).

Please answer from 1—strongly disagree to 5—strongly agree with 3 being neutral.

___ 28. I have dependable childcare.

___ 29. I would prefer not to work but am forced to by financial pressure.

___ 30. My job is emotionally satisfying.

___ 31. Being a father has a negative effect on my job security.

___ 32. I feel that my job serves an important purpose.

33. Does your company offer any kind of family-supportive programs?
(eg: subsidized childcare, flex-time, other alternative work schedules)

34. If you answered yes on #33, have you taken advantage of any or all of these programs? (If yes, please name which ones).

Table 7:
Fathers' Attitudes toward Work and Home

	Mean
Career	
Importance of advancement	3.50
Fatherhood affects job security negatively	1.83
Number of Work Hours	
Average hours worked before first child	47.50
Average hours you work now	50.00
Average hours wife worked before first child	41.67
Average hours wife works now	26.67
Time off for first child	16.33
Time off for second child	9.82
Company offers family supportive programs	1.42
Takes advantage of these programs	1.43
Job Satisfaction	
Job is emotionally satisfying	4.00
Feels job serves important purpose	4.83
Financial Needs	
Your income	57,595.00
Your wife's income	14,351.11
Pay is essential to my family	4.75
Income allows for quality childcare	3.92
Prefer not to work, but must for financial reasons	3.33
Effects of Mother Working	
Impact of mother's employment on child's well-being	3.33
Impact of mother's employment on child's schoolwork	3.50
Impact of mother's employment on child's cognitive dev.	3.33
Impact of mother's employment on child's emotional dev.	3.33
Childcare	
I have dependable childcare	4.33
Husband's Attitude	
Husband prefers wife to work	2.75
Wish dad spent more time with me	3.75
Gender Attitudes	
If both parents work full-time, childcare split equally	4.17
If both parents work full-time, housework split equally	4.08
What percentage of childcare are you doing	35.42
What percentage of childcare is your husband doing	64.58
Father's role is to put family first	4.08
Mother's role is to put family first	4.17
Demographics	
How many children do you have	2.33
Age of first child	76.00 months
Age of second child	48.60 months
Age of third child	61.00 months
Age of fourth child	60.00 months
Age of fifth child	36.00 months
Married	92%
Divorced	8%
Number of years you have been married	9.08
Age	35.00
Level of education	some college
Race	white

Responses were on a five point scale with 5 being highest, 3 being neutral and 1 being the lowest rating.
N=12

Table 8:
How a Mother's Employment Will Affect Her Child's
School Performance, Cognitive Development, and Emotional Development
According to the Father

	Negative Effect	No Effect	Positive Effect
Child's Well Being	16.7%	41.7%	41.7%
Child's Performance	8.3%	41.7%	50.0%
Child's Cognitive Development	8.3%	50.0%	41.7%
Child's Emotional Development	8.3%	58.3%	33.3%

N=12

Second Interview Questions for Mothers and Fathers[47]

1. How many children do you have?
2. What are their names/ages? Briefly describe each.
3. Do you think being a parent has changed you as a person? If so, how?
4. Do you think being a parent has changed your spouse? If so, how?
5. Has your arrangement for sharing housework changed from how it was split before you had children? (Housework includes typical cooking, cleaning, lawn care, home and repairs, etc.) If so, how? (Eg. Have responsibilities for chores become more fixed?) How was this decided?
6. On a scale of 1 to 10, how satisfied are you with this arrangement? If you could change anything about it, what would it be?
7. Can you describe how you and your spouse are dividing and sharing parenting responsibilities? (Take me through a typical day) How was this decided?
8. On a scale of 1 to 10, how satisfied are you with this arrangement? If you could change anything about it, what would it be?
9. Have you had any difficulties in sharing child care?

10. Overall, what percentage of the parenting and childcare are you doing and what percentage is your spouse doing? (eg. 50-50, 75-25)
11. Please comment on about how each of the following were handled eg. Mom 60%
    ♦ Night feedings (please comment on sleep deprivation)
    ♦ Sick days off work for child
    ♦ Diaper changing
    How did you arrive at this arrangement?
12. Have there been any problems with negotiating who does what with housework/childcare?
13. Do you feel like the present situation is fair for both of you?
14. Most couples at one time or another experience some conflicts over parenting. On a scale of 1 to 10 (1 meaning no conflict, 10 meaning a lot), how much conflict do you experience over parenting?
15. What would you be most likely to have conflict about?
16. You said you two were going to have _____ work arrangement.
Is that what you all ended up doing? Are you still doing it that way?
17. Are you happy with the arrangement?
18. How many hours a week do you work? (briefly describe your job)
19. How do you feel about your job?
20. How much do you like it? How involved are you? How successful do you feel?
21. How does your work life affect your family life? How does your family life affect your work life?

22. How many hours a week does your spouse work? Do you two make about the same income or who makes more? Much more?
23. How does your spouse's job affect your family life?
24. Who cares/cared for the children while you work(ed)?
25. Are you satisfied with your child care arrangements?
26. Who makes child care arrangements (day care, babysitter, etc.)? Always? Most of the time? Etc.
27. In general, is your family/work life going the way you expected it to go before you had children? Explain
28. Do you expect the division of child, house and work responsibilities to change in the future?
29. How could your (and your spouse's) work be more supportive of your family life?
30. Would you say that your husband/wife is emotionally more, less or the same close to the children as you are?
31. Who and what have influenced your perspective and desires on paid work, housework and childcare?
32. Where or from whom have you learned the most about being a parent?
33. How do you go about getting what you want and need?
34. In a typical week, would you have more, less, or about the same amount of leisure time (e.g., reading, exercising, watching TV, going out with friends) as your spouse?
35. How many hours do you sleep on a typical night?
36. (For stay at home parents) Do you miss working?
    If so, what aspects?
    If not, why not?
37. (For working people). Do you wish you were not working?

If so, what aspects?

If not, why not?

38. Is your spouse supportive of your working and your career? In what ways does s/he communicate his support?

Everyone

39. Would you like to have more children? Why/why not?
40. Are there ways that having children has made you closer to your spouse?
41. Are there ways that having children has put distance between you and your spouse?
42. Has money or finances figured into difficulties in family life?
43. What are you most likely to complain to your friends about?
44. Do you ever get criticism from any source about the way you are doing things? Praise? From whom are you likely to receive those messages?
45. There has been a lot of research recently about what is going on in the American family. Lots of changes have occurred in the last 20 years. Most women now work outside the home but are still responsible for most of the parenting. (Choose question that fits the participant.)

75-25 In your family, the mother is the primary parent. What is the most important reason that childcare is divided that way?

60-40 You/your husband does more than the average father. How would you explain that? The flip side of the question is why does the mother still do more?

50-50./alternating shifts. Why is your family different than the norm?

46. What advice would you give parents expecting their first child?

47. Is there anything I have left out or that you want to add?

NOTES

Introduction

[1] Both Freud and Marx addressed the needs adults have that are met through work. These are discussed in detail in Chapter 6: "Competing Demands: Work and Family."

[2] See chapter 4 for more examples of issues new parents need to consider.

[3] Certainly there are times when the child's parents are in a committed relationship without marriage. However, for brevity's sake, spouse will be used throughout the text to refer to the child's other parent.

[4] The term ME-WE-ME—as well as the interpretation and application of Bowen's Family Systems Theory in this introduction—were shamelessly stolen from my husband, Christopher Stanley-Stevens, a Licensed Marriage and Family Therapist at Tarleton State University.

[5] See Jerry Lewis' books, *No Single Thread* and *How's Your Family*, for more information on how power imbalances in marriages affect the development of children.

[6] John and Julie Gottman, John Bradshaw, Pepper Swartz and Fran Deutsch have all done extensive research on factors related to satisfying marriages and they all conclude that equally shared power is a necessary ingredient. Shared power is discussed in chapter 4.

Chapter 1

[7] While the book reports on 186 surveys and interviews, this chapter analyzes a subset of twenty-five surveys and fourteen interviews. The conclusions drawn here have been confirmed and supported by the experiences of students and workshop participants as well as by other research over the ten years since the first interviews.

[8] This average excludes a high school coach whose baby was due in May. Since he works a nine-month school year, his parental leave appeared to be forty-two days. When he was included, the average was 9.3 days.

[9] An interesting side-note: When wives made more money than husbands, the men were more likely than their wives to say that they were dual providers (versus saying she was the primary breadwinner). In contrast, when the wives made less than their husbands, they tended to name their husbands as the primary breadwinners rather than say they were dual earners. These responses reflect the cultural norm of thinking of men as the breadwinners.

[10] See Bahr (1982) as well as Hare-Mustin, Bennett and Broderick (1983).

Chapter 2

[11] I surveyed a total of 63 women and 22 of those women agreed to in-depth interviews. The questionnaires for the survey and interviews are provided in Chapter 10. Among those surveyed, 70.1 percent worked at least 31 hours a week before their pregnancies and 48.4 percent planned to work at least that much after their babies are 6 months old (see Table 1 in Chapter 10).

[12] Several students assisted me in this research project. They are named in the acknowledgements of this book.

[13] I took this concept from Russo (1979). More recently, Judith Warner (2005) described how upper-middle class moms were taking this to an extreme in, "Mommy Madness," the cover story of *Newsweek*.

[14] Of course, children do suffer if one or both of their parents work an excessive number of hours. Such problems are discussed in Chapter 5 on work. The point, here, is that some people assume that mother's working hurts the children while father's working doesn't.

[15] Kathleen Gerson (1985) provides a detailed discussion of job satisfaction and motherhood in her excellent book, *Hard Choices: How women decide about work, career and motherhood.*

[16] Our culture's norm that says that a father should be the primary breadwinner in the family was apparent with respect to how women and men answered the question of who was the primary breadwinner. When the women made more money, they would claim themselves as the primary breadwinner but their husbands would say they were dual providers. However, when the women made less money, both they and their spouses viewed the husband as the primary breadwinner.

[17] The traditional model for the workplace in the United States is one where the family is expected not to interfere. Consequently, in many organizations, supervisors tend to view parents missing work because of a sick child or a school event as a lack of organizational commitment and will give promotions to workers who do not "prioritize" their families. See Shea (2002) and Waldfogel (1997) for further discussion.

Chapter 3

[18] See Strong, B., DeVault, C.& Cohen, T. (2011).

[19] See Lamanna, M. & Riedmann, A. (2009) and Kiecolt-Glaser, J.K. & Newton, T.L. (2001).
[20] Munsey, C. (2009).

Chapter 4

[21] Huber, J. and Spitze, G. (1983).
[22] See Lamanna, M.A. & Reidmann, A. (2009).
[23] See Lamanna, M.A. & Reidmann, A. (2009).

Chapter 5

[24] See Pina, D.L.,& Bengston, V.L. (1993).
[25] See Radin, N. and Graeme, R. (1982).
[26] See Lovekin, K. (2003).
[27] See Bird, C.E. (1999), Kiecolt-Glaser, J.K. & Newton, T.L. (2001), and Lamanna, M.A. and Riedmann, A. (2009).
[28] See Lino, M. (2002).
[29] Coontz, Stephanie (1992).
[30] For more on what families were actually like in the 1950s, read *The way we never were* by Stephanie Coontz.

Chapter 6

[31] The University of Connecticut's Center for Survey Research and Analysis, "2000 report on U.S. Working Time" found 46% of workers working 41 hours or longer; 18% 51 hours or longer.
[32] Hochschild, Arlie. (2001).
[33] Deutch, F. (1999). .
[34] Lamanna, M.A. and Riedmann, A. (2009).
[35] See Williams, Joan, (2000).

[36] U.S. Department of Labor, Bureau of Labor Statistics (www.data.bls.gov), and Bianchi, S.M., & Casper, L.M. (2000).

[37] U.S. Census Bureau (2008).

[38] See Hochschild (2006).

Chapter 7

[39] See, for instance, Signorielli, N. (1998).

[40] Baker, R. (2003).

[41] Heintz-Knowles, K. (2001).

[42] Brooks, M. (2005).

Chapter 8

[43] See Lewis's books, *No single thread* and *How's your family?*

Chapter 9

[44] The average cost to raise a middle class child born in 2001 to age 18, before college, is $231,470 (Lino, 2002).

[45] Love, B. (2010). Interview with Chris Rock. Why I love . . . New York City. *Arrive Magazine.* May/June.

Chapter 10

[46] Many of these questions were adopted or adapted from Gerson (1985) *Hard choices: How women decide about work, career and motherhood.*

[47] Some questions are adapted from Deutsch, Francine (1999), *Halving it all: How equally shared parenting works.* Harvard.

REFERENCES

Abrams, D.C. (2002). Father nature: The making of a modern dad. *Psychology Today.* March/April, 38-47.

Bahr, H.M. (1982). Religious contrasts in family role definitions and performance; Utah Mormons, Catholics, protestants, and other. *Journal for the Scientific Study of Religion, 21*(3), 200-217.

Baker, R. (2003). *The awful truth.* Review of the great unraveling: Losing our way in the new century by Paul Krugman. *New York Review of Books* November 6, L, 17.

Bianchi, S.M., & Casper, L.M. (2000). American families. *Population Bulletin 55(4).* Washington DC: Population Reference Bureau.

Bird, C.E. (1999). Gender, household, and psychological disease: The impact of the amount and division of housework. *Journal of Health and Social Behavior,* 40:32-45.

Bowen, M. (1993). Family therapy in clinical practice. New York, NY: Aronson.

Bradshaw, J. (1990). *Bradshaw on: The family: A new way of creating solid self-esteem.* Deerfield Beach, FL: HCI.

Brooks, M. (2005). *The American family on television: A chronology of 121 shows, 1948-2004.* New Jersey: McFarland & Co.

Capizano, J, Tout, K. & Adams, G. Child Care Patterns of School-Age Children with Employed Mothers. (2001) Report of the Urban Institue. [on-line] Available February 14, 2001, at http://www.newfederalism.urban.org/html/op41.html#childcare.

Coontz, S. (1992). *The way we never were: American families and the nostalgia trap.* New York, NY: BasicBooks.

Deutsch, F. M. (1999). *Halving it all: How equally shared parenting works.* Cambridge, MA: Harvard.

Gerson, K. (1985). *Hard choices: How women decide about work, career, and motherhood.* Berkeley, CA: University of California Press.

Gottman, J. & Silver, N. (2004). *The seven principles for making marriage work.* London: Orion.

Hare-Mustin, R.T., Bennett, S.K., & Broderick, P.C. (1983). Attitudes toward motherhood: Gender, generational, and religious comparisons. *Sex Roles,* 9(5), 643-661.

Hendrix, H. (2001). *Getting the love you want: A guide for couples.* Owl Books.

Heintz-Knowles, K. (2001). Balancing acts: Work-family issues on prime-time TV in *Television and the American family,* second edition. Bryant, J and Brayant, J.A. (eds.) Maywah, NJ: Erlbaum.

Hochschild, A.R. (2001). *Time bind: When home becomes work and work becomes home.* New York, NY: Metropolitan.

Hochschild, A.R. (2006) Chapter 41: The nanny chain in *Inequality reader: Contemporary & foundational readings in race, class, & gender,* 357-360.

Huber, J. and Spitze, G. (1983). Sex stratification: Children, housework, and jobs. New York: Academic Press.

Kiecolt-Glaser, J.K. & Newton, T.L. (2001). Marriage and health: His and hers. *Psychological Bulletin,* 127:472-503.

Lamanna, M. & Reidmann, A. (2009). *Marriages and families: Making choices in a diverse society.* Tenth Edition. Belmont, CA: Wadsworth.

Lewis, J.M. (1979). *How's your family? A guide to identifying your family's strengths and weaknesses.* New York, NY: Brunner.

Lewis, J.M. (1976). *No single thread: Psychological health in family systems.* New York: Brunner/Mazel.

Lino, M. (2002) Expenditures on children by families, 2001" *Annual Report.* Washington DC: U.S. Department of Agriculture. Center for Nutrition Policy and Promotion.

Love, B. (2010). Interview with Chris Rock. Why I love . . . New York City." *Arrive Magazine.* May/June: 100.

Lovekin, K. (2003) When dads clean house, it pays off big time. UC Riverside sociologists say men likely to have better behaved children and wives who find them more sexually attractive. *Brain and Behavioral Sciences* no. 98 (June 8).

Macionis, J.J. (2008). *Sociology.* Twelvth Edition. Englewood Cliffs, NJ: Prentice-Hall, Inc.

Morris, H. J. (2001, September 3). Happiness explained. *U.S. News and World Report.* pp. 46-55

Munsey, C. (2009). Writing about wounds. *Monitor on psychology,* 40(9), 58.

Parcel, T.L. & Menaghan, E.G. (1994). *Parents' jobs and children's lives.* New York, NY: A. de Gruyter.

Pina, D.L., & Bengston, V.L. (1993) The division of household labor and wives' happiness-ideology, employment and perceptions of support. *Journal of Marriage and Family* 55: 901-912.

Radin, N. & Graeme, R. (1982) Increased father participation and child development outcomes. In *Nontraditional families: Parenting and child development*, ed. M.E. Lamb, Hillsdale, NJ: Erlbaum.

Russo, N.F. (1979). Overview: Sex roles, fertility and the motherhood mandate. *Psychology of Women Quarterly*, 4(1), 7-15.

Schwartz, P. (1994). Modernizing marriage. *Psychology Today*, September/October, 54-59.

Shea, R.H. (2002). The new insecurity. *U.S. News $ World Report*, March 25, 40.

Signorielli, N. (1998). Television and the perpetuation of gender-role stereotypes". *AAP News,* February, 7-10.

Strong, B., DeVault, C. & Cohen, T. (2011). *The marriage and family experience: Intimate relationships in a changing society. Eleventh Edition.* Belmont, CA: Wadsworth.

United States Census Bureau. www.census.gov

Waldfogel, J. (1997) The effect of children on women's wages. *American Sociological Review 62,2.* 209-17.

Williams, Joan, (2000). *Unbending gender: Why family and work conflict and what to do about it.* Oxford University Press.

Warner, (2005). Mommy madness. *Newsweek,* February 21.

ACKNOWLEDGEMENTS

Conducting this research and writing this book have been daunting tasks and I could have never done it without help from many people. My heartfelt gratitude is extended to all of the people named below and to the many others I've thanked along the way.

First, let me thank the 88 parents who participated in this study, sharing their perspectives for us all to learn from. And an extra big thank you goes to the 27 parents of young children who put in the time for two interviews and two surveys over the five year period of this study. Their names have been changed, as well as some identifying characteristics (for example, sometimes their occupations were changed to similar ones and sometimes the gender of their children were changed) in order to preserve their anonymity. Also, we made the couples' names alliterate in order to make it easier for readers to keep the couples straight in their minds.

Tarleton State University provided grant monies and a faculty development leave for this project. My department head, Lori Anderson, and colleagues Jason LaTouche and Carol Key worked together to make the faculty development leave a reality.

Regarding the first phases of surveys and interviews, I am most indebted to Reed Trosper and Karen Griffith.

Additionally, I want to thank the rest of the research team for their assistance with surveying, interviewing, and analyzing the results of our first time expectant parents: Mary Perkins, Kelly Talbot, Jerald Germany, Tiffany Lambert, Lena Cooley and Darlene Stephenson. Since there is not a list of first time expectant parents, this research team was crucial in identifying and recruiting our participants.

Teresa Williamson did most of the leg work involved in tracking down the original participants—most of whom had moved—five years later. Michele Ellis and Carmen Snyder aided in the transcription of these second interviews.

Jason LaTouche and Josh Hart read large portions of the book and provided feedback and Kathryn Jones did a wonderful job editing. Rachel and John Stanton provided feedback for the early chapters and Emily Burks made contributions to chapter 7.

I so appreciate the many friends who provided encouragement and feedback, and Alana Lennie who believed in this project and made important suggestions.

Parker and Forrest are the reasons I got interested in parenting in the first place. They have made me an enthusiast for the joy of parenting.

Most of all, I want to thank Christopher, who has tremendous insight into relationships and who has supported and encouraged me all of the way through this project.

Articles Related to this Research

Stanley-Stevens, L. and Kaiser, K. (2009). "Work and Family Decisions of First Time Expectant Mothers: A Causal Analysis." Presented at the Annual Meetings of the International Sociology Association, Oslo, Norway, June 15.

*Interviewed by Ruth Mancina (2009). "Baby 101," *Saginaw Valley Family Magazine.* April, 12-13.

*Stanley-Stevens, L. (2008). "What They Didn't Expect When They Were Expecting," *Family* magazine, February, 14-15.

Stanley-Stevens, L. (2008). "What They Didn't Expect When They Were Expecting: A Time Series Analysis of Mothers." Presented at the Pacific Sociological Association's Annual Meetings, Portland, OR, April 12.

Stanley-Stevens, L. & Seward, R. R. (2007) "Role Expectations of First Time Expectant Fathers," *Free Inquiry in Creative Sociology,* 35, 2, 57-72. (Published by Oklahoma State University)

Stanley-Stevens, L. & Seward, R. R. (2007) "First Time Expectant Fathers' Attitudes, Actions and Well Being in Regard to Family Issues," *Women's Health and Urban Life* Special Issue on Families and Well Being, VI, 2, 81-96. (Published by the University of Toronto.)

Interviewed by Whitney White-Ashley (2007). "Coping with Stress during the Holidays," *Area Wide Business & Commerce Journal,* 11: 8-9.

*Available online by joining the Facebook group called, "What They Didn't Expect When They Were Expecting."

INDEX